The Confessions of an Inept Love Soldier

by

Olwen Cowling

Published in the United Kingdom

Copyright © Olwen Cowling 2016
www.getyourboo.com

All rights reserved. No portion of this book may be reproduced, stored in a retrieval system or transmitted at any time or by any means mechanical, electronic, photocopying, recording or otherwise, without the prior written permission of the publisher.

The right of Olwen Cowling to be identified as the author of this work has been asserted by her in accordance with the Copyright, Designs and Patents Act 1988.

A CIP record of this book is available from the British Library

First printed August 2016

Cover artwork by Milliprint Ltd

ISBN 978-0-9955549-0-0

Dedicated to all the Love Soldiers

Keep believing

Contents

Lessons in Life

Why?
page 3

Pubes
page 7

Virgin
page 24

Condom
Page 40

Drunk
Page 58

No
Page 81

Wrong
Page 106

Lessons in Dating

Fish
Page 129

Safe
page 148

Blind
page 160

Short
page 178

Drugs
Page 194

Thick
Page 205

Fairy Tale?
page 217

Conqueror
page 241

Acknowledgements
page 245

Love Soldier:

> *Someone hoping for and/or looking for love.*

Love Conqueror:

> *Someone who has found reciprocated love, often after a bloody long search and/or wait.*

Lessons in Life

Why?

One beige Friday night, I got chatting online to a chap through plentyoffish.com. For the first time since Frank, I felt a genuine connection with someone through a dating site. He only had one picture on his profile. It was taken at a wonky angle and he was clutching a pack of Marlboro Lights. If you looked especially carefully, you could see a can of lager next to him. Hardly long-term material. He did, however, pick up nicely on the hint I'd included on my own dating profile page about my love for watching *You've Been Framed!* This was a huge bonus, as most of the first-contact messages I received were just 'Hi' or someone asking if they could cum in my hair. He drew my attention to his favourite clip ever. It was called 'Dog on a Swing'. I watched it. It was a clip of a dog swinging on a swing. A great choice. No one seriously hurts themselves and no one vomits.

Over the next two weeks, Jambo81 and I bantered back and forth. He had a job, he had teeth – and he, too, did not understand why people ate lemon curd. Most importantly, he made me smile when I got a message from him. Still, I was in the zone of understanding that this was as good as it got, and that made me like him without the pressure of wondering whether I should be feeling any more or any less. I had no intention of meeting up with him. He definitely didn't seem like a solid, long-term option. However, after a while, he suggested meeting up. He wanted to go to the greyhound racetrack. I pointed out that either of us could be psychotic, so perhaps agreeing to travel fifteen miles in a car together down a single carriageway was a bit risky for a first date. He then suggested a pub quiz. I found myself agreeing. What could go wrong?

The thing about having a successful date is that it doesn't matter what you do. You just need two open-minded people willing to get to know each other and able to keep an open view of what might come out of it. Oh, and you both need to turn up.

The night before the day we were due to meet, I received the following text:

`'I'm sorry, it's not you, it's me. I just can't meet you.'`

And that was that. I didn't even reply. He never contacted me again. Nothing. Not even to see if I was ok or to change his mind or to stress that it was his issues and nothing I had done. I was officially a dating leper – I was now being dumped by people who hadn't even met me yet.

That weekend, I sat contemplating life with my friend Lisa. It was another beige day: Sunday afternoon this time. I wondered whether finding true, Earth-shattering love was ever going to be my destiny. I wondered if the concept of True Romantic Love was starting to become a fairy tale myth personified. I was entering my fifth dating wilderness year. From the age of twenty-five onwards, all the dates, meetings, relationships and encounters I'd embarked on had gone tits up. Many within a few days, some after a couple of months, but a fair few within around forty-five minutes.

I was starting to believe that even if a knight in shining armour did gallop out of the mist to come and rescue me, his horse would probably shit all over my front garden.

My love life hadn't always been a disaster. By the age of twenty-one, I'd thought I had my attitudes and understanding of love and relationships pretty much sewn up. The funny thing about life is that you never know what might be lurking around the corner to challenge your core beliefs.

Don't get me wrong: I can't profess to be some self-righteous angel who was being mysteriously wronged by streams of men. Oh no. I made some hugely questionable choices and behaved pretty badly on a few occasions, too. Nevertheless, there I was: on the brink of completely giving up. In many ways, though, I had a newfound peace with love. I didn't give up the search but instead wondered if I just needed to tone down my expectations. Maybe True Love was just something created by Mills & Boon novels and Clinton cards. Film has a lot to answer for, too. Ooh – and comic books. Bloody Spider-Man. Have you seen the first film? Kissing upside down in the rain. It is unrealistic on so many levels. No one (apart from those involved in some seriously specific kink) would find having gallons of water poured up their nose sexy when trying to have a good kiss. Also, he is essentially part spider. What is the first rule of getting rid of a spider you find in your bath? Pour a shitload of water onto it.

So was love in its purest romantic form nothing more than an impossible goal after all? Perhaps the best thing I could ever hope for was companionship with a chap that I wanted to see naked on a regular basis. I was genuinely fine with it. Once I came to terms with my lowered expectations, it felt like a huge weight had been lifted from my shoulders.

But I still wondered: had I been kidding myself all of those times that I thought I was madly in love? And when did I start getting it all so sodding wrong?

Pubes

From as early in my life as I can remember, being in love and being loved in return was my goal. Don't worry – I am not going to launch into a tale of horrific sexual abuse. This story is a little lighter-hearted than that. Well, it has its moments. What I mean is that from an early age I was enthralled by tales of romance in books, in songs and most of all in films. I'd sit cross-legged on the carpet in front of the TV and be completely enchanted by Gene Kelly tap-dancing into the heart of some impossibly tiny-waisted lady, or by Maria – bowl haircut and all – getting together with Captain von Trapp. Even when the Betamax started to fail me, I would kneel beside it, finger on the play button, watching Maria look into Georg's eyes in soft focus as the Ländler played. I still feel that Christopher Plummer's Austrian suit is partly to blame for my fleeting desire for an older man.

    Now, I know that some people aspire to find love in the hope of one-day emulating affections that their parents showed to each other. I am not sure if that was the case with me. Maybe a little bit. My folks are still together and there is no divorce planned. Yet. How do I put it? We are not a fluffy family. We never concerned ourselves with outpourings of affection for each other. The other week I told my mum that I loved her. She replied: 'And I'm very fond of you, too.'

Ouch.

That's not to say that she doesn't love me back. We have developed a code. Have you ever seen the film *Ghost*? Well, if you haven't, you should. Once you've got over Demi Moore's haircut, it's a cracking film. Anyway, the point is that the Swayze never says 'I love you' back to bowl-cut Demi. Instead, he always replies 'Ditto'. We have something similar. Mum will say 'BYD'. The explanation being that once, Grandad used the phrase 'But you do' on a home video. It came to symbolise the notion that you think you might not cope with a situation, 'but you do'. This was shortened to BYD and eventually became a term of endearment.

No, I don't really get it either. But I do know that I like it and that hearing it always makes me feel better.

We are definitely not a family that thrives on huge public displays of affection. I have never seen them kiss each other in public. Not once. On the other hand, they unknowingly reveal glimpses of their affection for each other. They always give each other birthday and anniversary cards. They never do that modern-world thing of watching different TV programmes in separate rooms. They always sit next to each other on the sofa. They go to bed at the same time. Dad always gets up first and makes them both a cup of tea.

On reflection, I believe my folks have it spot on. Subconsciously, from as early as I can remember, I wanted to have a marriage like my parents have. The moment I start to go to bed earlier than a boyfriend, you know not to buy a hat for the wedding.

So, aside from my parents and musicals, what else shaped me at the beginning? Well, two weeks after my eighth birthday, I started boarding school. No, it wasn't because my folks wanted me gone at the earliest opportunity due to my incessant ice-skating using two *Beano* annuals and a tiled floor. Dad worked abroad. I was at the local international school but there was an awful lot of civil unrest. In the summer of my eighth birthday, the school was bombed. It didn't stop there. The school did not have fire drills. It had bomb drills. So, a year earlier than planned, I headed back to the UK to start boarding school.

I wasn't totally alone. I did have an older brother and sister there. Both were popular and didn't pander to me. I was the only boarder in my year group – for two whole years. Luckily, as there were hardly any boarders, the years mixed and I spent a lot of time with the girls in the year above me.

We had some good times but it was nothing like I had imagined. I totally blame Malory Towers for that. Nowadays, thanks to Harry naffing Potter, people's images of boarding school are even more warped. In fairness, boarding school nowadays is probably very different to how it was thirty years ago – although any suggestion of wands would be a child safety issue on more than one level. I am not sure if my school even had a child safety policy. I have a vague memory of a ChildLine poster above the only payphone we had access to, but you would never have dreamt of dialling the number. At the time, ChildLine to my mind was a telephone number that children who were being intentionally starved by their parents were encouraged to call. It was something occasionally mentioned by Esther Rantzen on *That's Life!*, in between presentations of amusing potatoes shaped like willies.

So should we have had more protection back then? Nowadays, a child being left alone, even momentarily, with a staff member without a truly solid reason and an encyclopaedia-sized book of signed approval forms would be considered 'a bit dodgy'. In those days, not so much. On reflection, though, there was some seriously questionable behaviour going on.

Within the first few days of boarding school, you had to have a medical. Ugh. Just the word 'medical' makes me feel like I want to sew knickers to my jeans up and lock the front door. No one, not even my housemistress, explained to me what a medical was. I was just told to walk down to the sanatorium after breakfast and wait. The matron opened the door. She ushered me into a little side room. There, she gave me a dressing gown and told me to take off all my clothes apart from my pants and put the dressing gown on. She told me that when I was ready, I had to go out and sit in the corridor and wait to be called through. It was almost deathly quiet and I was terrified. As I was the only female boarder to start that year, I was on my own. There I sat, eight years old and alone. I sat nervously in just my pants and that rank brown dressing gown, waiting to be called through to see the doctor. The sister called me through. She wasn't the maternal, bosomy type that you might have expected – she was solid, with a severe haircut, and had this unnerving habit of taking a sharp breath inwards whenever you said anything to her. I was ushered into the doctor's room. The sister stood by the door and the doctor told me to sit down. He was smartly dressed in a grey three-piece suit and had a deep Scottish accent. He seemed jolly enough and I started to feel at ease. Phew. I started to relax a bit as he went through general health questions. I had been in hospital when I was very little with severe asthma, so many of the questions revolved around that. I knew the drill and went through my medications and triggers. Blah blah. He asked me to lie down on the bench so he could 'feel my tummy'. So far, so doctory. At that point, the phone rang and the sister left the room. As if in slow motion, the doctor slowly and calmly put his hands down the front of my pants. He kept them there for what felt like the best part of forever, ever so slightly moving them around. He was examining me. That's ok. I wasn't exactly sure what he was examining, but at the age of eight, I didn't even understand why they used a lollipop stick to help a sore throat, so who was I to argue? The door began to open and he swiftly removed his hands. Sister came back in the room. He scribbled in my notes and told me that I was fit and healthy and that I could go and get dressed.

    I genuinely didn't think that anything inappropriate had happened. I was just glad to be heading back to lessons knowing that the dreaded 'medical' was over. I do remember, however, that I never wanted to go back into that room ever again.

    Of course, I know now that he was a bit of a paedophile.

    Not that we weren't looked after on that front. I genuinely didn't believe there was anything dodgy about the medical, so didn't say anything. It never happened again, and to be honest, it was only when I got into my late-teens that I realised what had happened to me wasn't ok – although, in the eighties, I am not all that sure that if I had told someone I would have been taken seriously. He was a doctor. I was eight. Having said that, though, when it was mentioned to the French teacher that the PE teacher wanted to see if the girls' spines aligned correctly by getting them to bend over together, there was a meeting. It became apparent that he had also been 'touching (their) bottoms' (to quote a student in the meeting). Not long after, he 'mysteriously' disappeared.

Today, there is a huge emphasis in schools, particularly boarding schools, on well-being. Back then, not so much. In the eighties, it may as well have been called boreding school – we were always so bloody bored. The school I went to was even worse. It was a boarding school on its way out. It was more like a normal old-style grammar school with the addition of a few beds in a classroom above Room 1 for the few 'overnight students'. Our leisure time revolved around watching *Neighbours* at 5.35pm. Except for the hour of letter writing imposed on us on Sunday afternoons just after lunch, we were positively discouraged from contacting anyone. No fax, no phone calls – and of course, back then, no email or texts. Just a letter from my folks every two weeks. There was the aforementioned outgoing payphone situated next to a form room, but as we weren't ever given any money, it only ever seemed to be used to call the operator and give them a song. The only incoming phone was in the housemistress's living room. You couldn't exactly treat yourself and pop down there after lights out for a cry and a long-distance call while she was watching *Heart to Heart*.

My source of sanity and my friend to this day was Barky. (Not her birth name. Clearly.) Barkers was in the year above me. We would entertain ourselves. At weekends, we would pack a bag, each put a pair of (clean) pants on our heads, and 'run away'. In reality, we would head either for the girls' toilets in the Bedford block or for the trees next to the cricket pitch. We did try to erect a tent once. Barky brought it back after one half-term holiday. It did not go well. It was a four-man tent with no instructions. It was raining and we didn't have a hammer. Ok, so we couldn't even lay out the base correctly – but we had a brilliant time. We named the debacle 'The Raising of the Mary Rose' and I laughed so much that afternoon that I might have wet myself.

So, at this point you might be thinking that my need and search for love was probably down to something lacking in my childhood; down to early boarding school and no hugs. Maybe. But although I didn't have my parents around very much, I had some amazing friendships. The girls' dormitory was just one big room with a bed and a side table for each girl. There were around fifteen of us, ranging in age from me (at eight) through to twelve-year-olds. Despite the age differences and the day-to-day irritations, if anyone was ever upset or homesick, the others would rally round instantly. Often the tears would flow after lights out. If one person noticed, they would head to your bed and comfort you. Others would duly follow, like bees around a drooping sunflower. They did not leave until the tears stopped.

So, as surprising as it may sound, I felt very loved in those early days of boarding school. A couple of years went by. I was ten and doing fine. I worked fairly hard and was reasonably clever. People used to copy my French homework, so I can't have been all that bad. I would love to tell you about my first boyfriend. A sweet, puppy love, shared between two innocent children hand-holding on the way to the canteen. Not quite. If you ever doubted that I could be a bit tapped and questionably sad, this will confirm it. Some people invented girlfriends and boyfriends that they had 'at home' to make themselves look less like loners and more 'cool'. I managed to take that concept, run with it and succeed in making myself look like I had problems. At that time, I functioned partially in a fantasy world. Not so much inventing a boyfriend – more inventing a life. Not a realistic, attainable life, mind. Oh no. That would've been far too straightforward. No. I chose to submerge myself in a full-on romance with a chap I saw in what was a pretty average film. Yes, in my head I was married to Kevin Costner. Yep. Kevin

Costner. I saw *Robin Hood: Prince of Thieves* and I was smitten.

Honestly, my buttocks are so clenched and my anus so tight as I ponder the depths of my fabrication. I did my research. Man, if I had put half the effort into studying as I did into thinking about Kevin sodding Costner, I would be a brain surgeon by now. I will add that my imaginings were very chaste and innocent. The most sexual thing about it was the picture I had above my bed. And when I say above, I mean on the ceiling. It was a double-page picture from his film *No Way Out*. And it showed a nipple. Saucy.

You would think that I'd have been bullied to within an inch of my life for my behaviour. Even I would've been tempted to flush my ten-year-old self's head down the loo. But oddly, it was accepted. The school only had around three hundred students, so everyone knew who I was. As I was popular, I could get away with it. Everyone knew that I collected pictures of him. Students from other years in the school would hand me pictures they had found in their magazines. I had a Costner bible for the smaller pictures. Larger pictures were on the wall above my bed. Even the dinner ladies helped me out. One did a pirate video recording of *Robin Hood* for me. To this day, that is one of the nicest things anyone has ever done for me. On Sundays, the other full-boarders and I *would* watch it over and over again (partly because the only other films we had were *Elvira* and the first three episodes of *The Simpsons*).

Ah, but all good things (or creepy, inappropriate fixations) must come to an end. Funnily enough, it didn't take much to put me off Kev. I saw Michael Keaton in *Batman Returns* and thought he was better looking. That was that. Within days the pictures were off the walls. How superficial was I?

You know, I watched Robin Hood the other day. I was baffled. What was all that about? For a start, Kev has got a mullet. Then there is his accent, a sort of American / Canadian / Dick Van Dyke impression. Plus, he doesn't look particularly young. He was around thirty-three at the time. Hey ho. Creepy as it was, it was all innocent. After Kev, I had other crushes – but nothing on the scale of what I had felt for Kev Costner. Thank goodness. If I had, I probably should have been assessed. Michael Keaton was probably the closest. *Batman Returns*. It began my love for strong eyebrows on a man. It also ignited my inner goth, which (although very well hidden) remains.

It's lucky for some 'celebs' that things like Twitter and Instagram didn't exist when I was a teenager. There would have been some very gentle stalking from my younger self. In my adult life, I do still dabble. In fact, the only reason I joined Instagram was to have a peek into Michael Keaton's 'real life'. Sadly, apart from a couple of pics of his dog, it is just reams of political newspaper articles and evidence that he takes himself comically seriously. Have you seen the film *Team America*? You know, all that 'actors can save the world' bollocks. Another fantasy dashed. Saying that, I also follow Arnold Schwarzenegger. Arnie. Now him, I still would. Oddly, I don't go for hugely muscly men in general, but he is 'somink else' (sic). The way he is ripped, his accent, his height, his acting, him in a suit, him feeding deer ...[1] His Instagram shows you that he is everything that you would want him to be. Despite numerous heart operations and questionably dyed hair, I still very much 'would'. *Twins* was the first film I ever saw at the cinema. Even though I first saw it at the age of eight, I don't think I ever got over the scene where his biceps rip through his shirt. Ooh, and the shower scene. Hmm, I am going to stop this chat about Arnie's muscles as I could write an entire book on that alone, and I am already starting to feel a bit hot.

Yes, there were also 'real' boys that I fancied. In particular, there was a fellow boarder. There were only six full-time boarders, and he and I were two of them. He was like a mini Tom Cruise. Short and beautiful, and we got on incredibly well. It was a fleeting fancy that kicked off when

---

[1] The opening scene in *Commando* – honestly ...

the full-boarders were forced to go and see a slideshow about trains at a local village hall one Saturday night. Matron took us. Honestly, it was 1991 but you would have thought it was 1964. It was more a friendship love than anything, but it made a few weekends go a bit quicker.

There was also a boy I sat next to in history class. He had a Head brand bag with detachable football boots side bags. Cool. Our history teacher was a true sixties-style teacher and completely brilliant. He made us both sit at the desk directly in front of him because we were 'trouble', but really it was because we were his favourites in the class.

As for people fancying me? I am not sure that anyone ever did. I was tall and chubby. I had a giant smile and was always on good form which helped me be popular – but just as a friend. Never as a girlfriend. Having said that, there was one person. I can't quite remember his real name. Allegedly, he fancied me. He was also frightened of me. Hmm. Suddenly, in hindsight, I find myself wondering what issues that poor chap harboured. He was also the child who always cried at everything. You know – *that* one. The one who always had a slightly used hanky about their person.

I did, however, manage one 'boyfriend', although it was never called that. You would 'go out' with someone. I 'went out' with Dave. I thought he was amazing. I have no idea what he saw in me, but I suspect he just went out with me because he was bored. He had something of the young Michael J. Fox about him and was really funny. He would 'do' *Byker Grove*. This involved him jumping into the air and shouting 'By'er!' Ok, it's a visual thing, but for those of you who were around in 1990, you will know the credit sequence to *Byker Grove* that I am referring to and would've found it hilarious at the age of eleven. I don't remember how going out with Dave came about. My friend asked him out for me. I do remember that my fancying him became one of the worst-kept secrets in the school. Totally my own fault. I had sent him a Valentine's card earlier that year. By accident, I had started to sign my own name and panic-Tipp-Exed it out. All he had to do was scratch off the Tipp-Ex. Bugger.

Still, it was never going to work. He borrowed my red felt-tip once in prep and never gave it back. It wasn't long before he was going out with Sarah. Ah, Sarah. The kind of beauty that always looked like she had a little make-up on – but she was just naturally pretty. My chubby cheeks could not compete with that. Saying that, they didn't last too long. There were rumours she was only with him for the games at his dad's arcade. I know. Bitch.

At thirteen, I had to pack up my things at the junior school and start again – this time at one of the most exclusive girls' schools in the UK. For me, there were a few initial problems:

1) It was six times the size of my last school.
2) Most people were from cash-rich backgrounds and were fairly posh. I wasn't very posh. I wasn't very rich. Our fees were heavily supplemented through my dad's work.
3) Everyone was ridiculously clever.
4) The only penis was male teacher penis.

Well, I say there was only male teacher penis. There were 'socials' set up with nearby boys' schools. Ugh. The only thing less sociable than a girls' school plus a boys' school social is a black-and-white ball where only lions are invited and everyone decides to turn up dressed as a zebra.

Still, needs must when the hormones drive. Without much day-to-day male interaction, most of us occupied ourselves with slightly disturbing flirtations with the male members of staff. An English teacher who looked like Wayne Slob from *Harry Enfield & Chums* was lusted after by many. Although once the new art teacher turned up, he was knocked off the pedestal. People said this chap looked like Mulder from *The X-Files*. He didn't.

I loved Mr David. Well, I wasn't exactly in love with him. I'm not even sure I fancied him. I was just a bit bored. He looked a bit like Charlie from *Casualty*. Sadly (for him), he was the biology teacher. Anyone with the idea that teaching at a well-known all-girls' boarding school might be dull would be mistaken. We got up to many things. We asked to study reproduction so much that when he finally had to teach the topic, he stuttered whenever he had to say 'penis'. My favourite was tying him up in lab coats, putting antler ears on him and – when he resisted going into a cupboard – writing 'Mr David likes to do it after dark in the lab' on the blackboard and getting the lab technicians in to watch. They laughed and left him. Never fear – this isn't going to digress into an anecdote for Operation Yewtree. Saying that, one teacher did send one of my friends some romantic French literature for no given reason. He taught her economics.

The summer I turned sixteen was a big one for many reasons. I had come to the end of a very long GCSE exam period. Believe it or not, I worked genuinely hard for them. By the time June came around, I was ready for a break and champing at the bit. A break away from highlighter pens, those reminder cards, and feeling guilty for watching *EastEnders* because of an impending exam. Finally, the Holy

Grail that was GCSE leave came along. It was a four-week period in between GCSE exams finishing and the end of term. We were catatonic with excitement. I mean, it was folklore that a socialite ex-pupil had got pregnant while on GCSE leave. Wow. What delights could await us 'normal' folk?

Virgin

Brilliantly, my leave timed nicely with Euro 96. You know the song 'Summertime' by Will Smith? Well, for the UK, it wasn't so much the summer that year as the football itself that was the aphrodisiac. Even the most hardened anti-football people out there couldn't help getting swept up in all the excitement. 'Three Lions (Football's Coming Home)' became the soundtrack to some remarkable times. We all genuinely believed that England would win the tournament. I was fifteen, and things were starting to kick off for me with regard to boys/men/willies – however you want to put it. Yes, at fifteen I was young, but thanks to an August bank holiday birthday I was just a bit young for my school year. Most of my friends were around sixteen. Physically, I had started to blossom. My height was less of a hindrance and more of an asset and, due to a newfound love of cottage cheese when I was fourteen, I was a bit slimmer than I had been.

    I was one of the lucky ones. Although I went to an all-girls' school, I maintained friendships with some chaps from my old school, one of whom stayed my closest friend for many years. Luckily for me, Chris lived in a mega-house with his awesome family, who were happy to host a party or two. June 26th 1996 was, for many, a day of overwhelming disappointment. England narrowly missed out on a much-deserved place in the final. We slipped out on penalties. I, too, was disappointed – although less so after I had spent half an hour behind the hay bales with some guy in his mid-thirties in a leather jacket.

If you were very VERY lucky, your parents would reluctantly agree to let you go on a parent-free holiday. To this day, I am still amazed that I was allowed. (Perhaps I am more amazed because I know what we got up to.) Three of my closest friends and I booked five days in Newquay. It was bizarre, confusing, terrifying, and hilarious – all in equal measures. We had a flat that consisted of a room with two bunk beds and a kitchen/living room. We had high expectations of a luxury holiday when we read in the description of the flat that it was 'fully carpeted except kitchen area'. When we arrived and saw it, we felt a little misled. The kitchen area was six inches of flooring next to the cooker.

Rightly or wrongly, my attitude at that time towards sex and my virginity was that it was something to get out of the way. It was fairly common for people to head off on a GCSE leave holiday a virgin and head home less so. Sex on

GCSE leave was sort of a rite of passage (no pun intended) before starting your A-levels. I was fine with the idea of throwing away my virgin badge. There was no peer pressure; it was all me. I know that doesn't paint me in the best light, but if we are all honest with ourselves, a lot of us had the same thoughts about our virginity.

On our second night of GCSE leave in Newquay, I lost my virginity to a chap I met in a club. I specifically use the term 'lost my virginity', as I don't see how you could class it as 'having sex' for the first time. It was dark. He put it in. After a few thrusts, he farted. No, really. He farted. If losing your virginity to a man you probably couldn't now recognise in a line-up who farted after four hip thrusts wasn't bad enough, he actually made it worse. Instead of ignoring it, he said:

'Oops, sorry. Too many beans.'

shudder

The next day, I felt like a weight had been lifted. I had done 'it'. The mystery was over. It wasn't awful but it definitely wasn't great. I only hoped that it got a bit better than that. If that was what all the fuss was about, I probably could have waited. I would like to say that he was the only one that holiday but he wasn't. There was another. Maybe two. Who am I kidding? I know there was. Who knows why? It was as if because I had done it once, that was the bar set and that was what happened. A natural progression after a bit of snogging. In America, they say that unless you are mature enough to cope with having a baby, you aren't mature enough to have sex. I can sort of see the logic, but to be honest the population of the Earth would die out fairly quickly if we had to stick to that as a rule. Instead, I believe that if you believe in even one myth told to you that starts with 'you can't get pregnant if ...', you shouldn't be giving or receiving a penis in a vagina. I genuinely believed that you couldn't get pregnant while on your period. I came on my period while I was on holiday. Boy, did I take a risk. Yep. I took a proper risk underneath the stars, under some bushes. No condom. Ugh. I thought that as I was around my period being due, it would be fine. As it happened, I was fine. I know now that I was lucky. No one truly knows their cycle. It can happen anytime. The only way you can guarantee not getting pregnant is if you are already pregnant. You can plug away with your birth control and you can even avoid penetrative sex, but the reality is that if there is a chance that sperm can find an egg, you are risking maternity jeans.

    Believe it or not, I don't regret doing it then. I was lucky that all my encounters were pretty kind to me. I mean, even the guy who farted apologised. I was incredibly lucky in terms of personal safety, too. If I told you everything that happened during those few days in Newquay, you probably wouldn't believe me. If you did, you would wonder how on Earth I wasn't found stabbed behind a service station. I really (really really) stupidly got in the car of a chap I met. He was an American in the army. We drove back to his barracks. We sat on his bed and chatted and kissed. Things got a little heavier and I suddenly got scared. I should have just told him to get off me but I didn't. I was sort of frozen in the moment. For some reason I suddenly blurted out, 'I'm fifteen!' I can see his face now. He looked genuinely terrified and said, 'Oh man! I'm a cop!' He pulled away and I laughed. It was partly sheer relief and partly because I felt like I was in a scene from a bad 1980s American sitcom after-school special. I didn't believe him until he showed me his badge. Bloody hell. He was an American policeman. The brakes were put on anything we might have done. He then opened up and told me about a girl he had been seeing who had broken up with him recently. He missed her terribly and he let out all of his emotions. Not exactly what I was going back to his place for, but man, it was so much better. We talked and had a cup of tea. Then he drove me back to the holiday apartment. I will say that it was (almost) the last time I got into a stranger's car like that. I was fucking lucky.

It wasn't the last time I would do something stupid and put myself at unnecessary risk, but it stopped me from doing anything else so stupid on that holiday. It's a lesson you have to learn. No one can risk-assess your situations for you. You have to learn to do that yourself, especially when it comes to sex. In all honesty, I know I didn't particularly understand sex at the time. It's not that I was naive or sheltered. Quite the opposite. It's a cliché, but it felt like having sex gave me the affection that I craved. It felt like I held all the power. They wanted to have sex with me and I had the power to allow them. When I did, it made them happy. It's a shame, looking back. Don't get me wrong; I wasn't the local bike or anything, but I definitely went further than I probably wanted to on a few occasions. I needed to do some growing up in order to appreciate it. Hey ho. I got my virginity out of the way and that was that. It would be quite a while before I properly enjoyed it.

    I had one or two 'sort of' boyfriends between the ages of fifteen and seventeen, but nothing much. There was one that bothers me a bit. When I look back on it, he should probably be registered on List 99.[2] I was fifteen and stupid. He was married and working away from home. It went on for a month or two. I was such a moron. I would wait for him to contact me. If we were around other people, he wouldn't even look me in the eye. He had the ability to make me feel like a princess one minute and like a bag of crap the next. It's

---

[2] Sex Offenders' Register.

sad to admit, but I took it as a compliment that he wanted me. The reality is that whoever you are and whatever the circumstances are, if you are a bloke in your thirties having sex with a girl you know is fifteen, you're a paedophile.

    It wasn't all sex offenders. There was one sweet guy I saw for a few months. He was my own age, bright and attractive. It didn't really go anywhere. In fact, he came out to me as a born-again Christian not long after we went our separate ways, so I guess me and him were never going to be heading down the same path.

    I was seventeen when I got together with my first 'proper' boyfriend (you know – mix tapes, touching and things). His name was Jim. He went to the same university as my sister. How cool was I? I was seventeen and still at school, but I had a boyfriend at university. Admittedly, we had absolutely bugger all in common. No, really – nothing. Saying that, he had a superb body and could quote Jean-Claude Van Damme. Who knows, maybe this is all you need in a man? It was the first time I got to appreciate that sex was a two-way thing and not just a general expectation. I believed he cared about me at the time, as I did him. It was definitely my first understanding that affection wasn't just about bonking. It was also about just saying nice things and being missed. He bought me Alpen. Having those extra little bits in place makes all the difference.

Although it was my first experience of genuine affection, it was also my first experience that men can be real wankers. One weekend, I was staying with my sister. He was heading to a party but was only going to stay a couple of hours. Then he would be back. I believed him one hundred percent. Why wouldn't I? He rarely drank, and I was still fairly naive. It got to 9pm and he still hadn't turned up. Soon it was 11pm. I couldn't sleep. I was still half waiting for him to turn up on the doorstep. As the time ticked on, I became more and more despondent. He couldn't have been that bothered about me after all. I was hardly ever in London, yet he had chosen to piss off without me and leave me waiting. Instead of thinking that he was twenty, a man, and stupid, I thought it was me. I just wasn't interesting enough. Not sexy enough. He just didn't want me.

I lay there as 11pm became midnight and then 1am. I was wide awake. Wide awake enough to hear him – pissed as a fart – calling me from the street below. I wasn't going to let him in but I wasn't one for cutting my nose off to spite my face. I found myself not only letting him in but forgiving him. Yes. He leaves me hanging all evening feeling like a worthless turd, and he gets let off and given a blow job.

On the whole, though, he was a good guy. I once commented that I was a fatty. He told me that I wasn't, because 'I wouldn't go out with you if you were fat'. Maybe not the most PC thing to say, and possibly borderline offensive, but not to me. It was one of the nicest things anyone had ever said to me.

As we had got together in my last year of school and his final year of university, the writing was probably on the wall for us from the start. But it was nice to finally have a boyfriend, even if we only saw each other about six times in the whole six months or so that we were together – thanks to A-levels and boarding school and his commitments to his final year.

Before we parted ways, he did, however, accompany me to the Leavers' Ball at my school. Ah, the Leavers' Ball. Yes, I could be a doormat, but I definitely had my own mind. For some completely irrational and inexplicable reason, one of my missions that evening was to try and get a kiss from all the male members of staff. Yes, my boyfriend was there. Yes, he was confused. I have photographic evidence of my English teacher literally wrenching me off as I attempted to mount him. Others weren't so hesitant. You know that phrase 'It's all fun and games until someone gets hurt'? Well, in this case, it was all fun and games until the tech teacher tried to put his tongue in your mouth.

The day after the Leavers' Ball, I sat at the train station ready to wave Jim off. We made vague promises to stay together, but there and then we both knew it was imminently over. He was heading off to BumFuckNowhere to do whatever it was he did for work and I was off for a summer working in Cyprus before starting university in the September. You know, even if we hadn't been going our separate ways, I am not sure we would have ever recovered from the day he broke the news to me that Geri was leaving the Spice Girls.

Off to Cyprus I went. You would think this would mean working in a bar or as a holiday rep for six weeks of nonstop party fun. Um. Not quite.

As I mentioned earlier, my dad worked abroad. At that time, he was posted in Cyprus. The job I had wasn't quite Coyote Ugly waitress fun but was working in the administration department of his office. Not only was it unglamorous, but it involved starting work at 7.30am. The hours of work in Cyprus were generally early in the morning until mid-afternoon. This isn't too much of a problem for most workers. They would have a nice snooze in the afternoon and a long mezze meal in the evening. For me, it had slightly different implications. I wanted to go out in the evenings, and due to the meal culture, no bars got going until around midnight. Bear in mind I was starting work at 7.30am, and my dad was a manager. You can see the issues.

I didn't go out all that often until I met Michelle. Her mum was friends with my mum and they thought we would hit it off. Now, I had fallen foul of that ol' chestnut before, but on this occasion, Mum was spot on. We got on like a house on fire – a house that had been doused in vodka and then set on fire, to be more accurate. In Nicosia where we lived, there weren't many bars that were appealing to us Brits. But there was one: The Shamrock. It was frequented by people of all nationalities and by foreign workers, including soldiers and people out there working for the UN.

The first night that we went out together, Michelle set me up with a friend of the chap she was seeing. I honestly can't remember why, but I wasn't that interested in this guy. He was attractive and German (as you know, I have a soft spot for a Germanic accent), but it wasn't really working for me. He got a bit handsy, and I needed an escape route. For a brief moment, we were away from the guys we were with. Michelle and I were chatting together. Out of the corner of my eye, I noticed this tall, tanned chap. He was wearing a white t-shirt and a silver chain and was holding a can of beer. I made a bet with Michelle that he was an Aussie. She dared me to wander over and say to him 'You're Australian' and walk off. I did.

Not long afterwards, he came to talk to me. He smiled and said (adopt Australian accent in your head for this bit),

'How did you know?' He offered to look after me and keep Mr Handsy German at bay. Mr Australian was gorgeous. I was thrilled. Funnily enough, he said he had seen me the week before at a UN concert. He was convinced it was all a set-up and that I knew who he was. I really didn't. He just looked Australian. We got chatting. He was a policeman. An Australian policeman working on a peace mission for the UN. I shit you not.

We chatted more and then had a cheeky slow-dance snog to Tracy Chapman's 'Baby Can I Hold You?' It was getting late, and he offered to drive me home. We headed towards his car. A standard white UN vehicle. Well, actually, his car was next to it. A brand new black BMW. I'm not a car person, but I was impressed. We pulled up outside the house and talked for a while. Then kissed for a while. Then (and this is something that still makes me a little doe-eyed), he kissed the back of my neck in a way that I had never been kissed before. If it had been an eighties film, there would have at least been a few fireworks or a Catherine wheel in the distance. Ooh, and maybe there would have been some sort of running-along-the-beach montage, like in *Baywatch*.

That was it. I was smitten.

I let myself in at 5.45am, called to Mum that I was home safe, and popped my head on my pillow. For forty-five minutes. I had to be up at 6.30am in order to be at work for 7.30am. Painful, but worth it.

We didn't swap numbers then, as he didn't seem to have one and mine was my parents'. Luckily, the night I met him, Michelle mentioned going up to the Kangaroo Club a few days later. It was a social club mainly for the Australians posted there, but due to the type of work our respective parents did, Michelle and I were able to go. I remember seeing him standing there and having no idea what to do and how to act. He came over. It was fabulous. He stood talking to his colleagues with his hand around my waist. Man, I was fresh out of school, about to turn eighteen, and was sort of officially seeing a thirty-three-year-old Australian policeman working for a peacekeeping force. How sexy was that? After that evening at the Kangaroo Club, we sneaked up to the disused runway in his car to look at the stars. I say look at the stars. We clearly went up there to shag.

One thing that he did that I hadn't experienced before is that when he said he would call me, he called me. My first proper boyfriend was always a bit vague, so I hadn't got used to the concept that a man could say that he would do something and would then actually do it. I would get home from work; he would say he'd call at 2.30pm. Lo and behold, he did. The best of these calls was when he asked if I wanted to go to Ayia Napa with him and his friends for the weekend. Um. Yes? Ok, so some of you might be thinking: hang on – this chap was in his thirties, and I was only seventeen. In his defence, I was days away from my eighteenth birthday, and he didn't know I was quite as young as that. Well, not until I invited him to my eighteenth birthday party. You might also wonder why my parents were ok with all this. To be honest, they trusted me and, due to the nature of Mick's job, they trusted him. He was charming without being creepy charming, and he had the balls to come in and meet my folks when it was needed. Mum actively encouraged me to go. Never was an opportunity like that ever going to come up again, and she knew it.

It was like a fantasy. He picked me up in his BMW after work and we headed off to the apartment he was staying in with his friends for the weekend. Remember, this was 1998 – before Ayia Napa became chav- and vomit-tastic. Only serious clubbers and decent holidaymakers headed there, as it was still relatively expensive to get flights. There was this fantastic image that stays with me to this day. Five of us on the balcony of their apartment, drinking beer and chatting. Me in my black bikini, sitting on Mick's lap. His mates, all gorgeous in nothing but swimming shorts. All were charming and all were trying to convince me some shit

Australian band was decent by playing random tunes. His friends treated me like a sister and he treated me like a girlfriend.

We spent the day on the beach. Mick and I canoodled, seventies-style. Yes, this also meant having sex in the sea. We never did it on the sand. Apart from the risk of being arrested, why would you want to encourage sand in your lady garden? The evening was dinner, drinking and dancing. Good, clean fun. Well, clearly we went back to the apartment early for bonking, but other than that, it was good clean fun. Saying that, I do remember being woken up in the middle of the night by him trying to have more sex with me. It is a very strange, fairly unpleasant thing to wake up to. It's odd how something can be so beautiful one moment, and five hours later it can be rather rapey. Hmm. I never got a proper explanation, and he knew it had upset me. My little fantasy world cracked a little, and again I was reminded that men can be real dickheads.

I let it go. To be honest, I was still so new to the dating world that I wasn't that sure what was generally expected. So hey ho. We continued seeing each other, and he came along to my 'musicals'-themed eighteenth birthday party. He has since told me that while he was sitting on my bed as I painted sideburns on him (he was Kenickie from

Grease), he caught sight of my soft toys. At that moment, he did feel like a predatory paedophile.

Soon, September came around. Mick was heading back to Melbourne, and I was due to head off to start university life. To this day, I can recall our last meeting clearly. I asked him if he thought we would ever see each other again. He answered: 'If you want to see me again, you'll see me again'. He kissed me gently and drove off under the Nicosia stars.

Condom

I know that for many people, starting university was a big, scary prospect. The wrench of leaving the bedroom you grew up in. Being left to fend for yourself after countless mornings relying on your mum to get you out of bed in time for school.

If, like me, you had been at boarding school for ten years prior to university, getting there was everything you wished boarding school had been – and so much more. Just the idea that you could have all your booze out on display was so exciting. No more hiding your home-made bottles of Snake Bite behind boxes of Tampax.

From that very first night, I fitted right in. I've never had too many problems making conversation. I've never been an 'I think you'll find' person (You know, that person who unnecessarily corrects other people – often starting with the statement 'I think you'll find ...') and have always been self-deprecating. I have also always been up for most things. Sorry, again I sound like a bike, but what I mean is that if someone thought something sounded like a fun plan, I'd give it a go; I would happily climb a phone box, try and blow up a condom just by putting it over my head and blowing through my nostrils etc.

I had been allocated a room in a mini-flat in the only off-campus halls of residence. You know, I can't think of its name without remembering Charlie. It was fairly common for us to be woken up at 4am by his chant in the courtyard. It went as follows:

> *'Mary Chapman Court*
> *You're all a bunch of wankers*
> *Except for the ones I like*
> *The rest of you are twats'*

Catchy.

I didn't mind it. I was a heavy sleeper and he once told me that I was 'one of the ones he liked'.

So there we were. All settling into our self-contained little flats, each with the company of four other strangers. Being off-campus somehow gave us a greater bond and we all stuck together, seeking out city-centre pubs and clubs so that we didn't have to keep traipsing up to the campus bars.

I bonded well with girls and boys alike. I wasn't fussy about who I was friends with. If people were warm to me, I was warm back. Of course, there were the ones I learnt not to hang out alone with. One chap wanted to show me his artwork in his room. He was an amateur photographer. (I know. You can see where this is going, but I didn't.) They were all black-and-white shots of naked women, primarily in handcuffs and plastic gloves. No, I mean bondage plastic, not marigolds. He casually went through his 'portfolio' with me and then asked if I would mind posing for him. He sold it to me as 'an opportunity for me to have some classic nude shots to look back on when I am old and grey'. I just thought it was 'an opportunity for him to see my boobs'. I didn't see him much after that.

There are lots of scare stories out there about starting university and all the sexual expectations – the phrase 'fuck a fresher' has to have to come from somewhere. I can, in all honesty, say that it just wasn't like that for me and the group of people I hung about with. It was far more about general drinking games at the nearest pub, stealing massage parlour adverts from phone boxes, and contemplating what lectures we could get away with not going to.

It was all a fairly Benny Hill-style affair. Everyone had their drinking game nicknames. Mine was Miss Steed. I seem to remember it was because I had a Bond Girl t-shirt on during one drinking game and that developed into *The Avengers* and Miss Steed sounded better than Mrs Peel. I don't know. It makes less sense the more I type about it. My favourite nickname was Pervy Pete. Poor bloke. On the very first night he was helping a girl into a dodgem car and he grabbed her boob by mistake (so he said), although it stuck even more a few days later when he was in one of the girls' flats and he somehow managed to trip over a thong.

After losing my virginity back when I was fifteen, I had definitely already learnt that there is a greater power in holding things back than opening your legs to anyone who came knocking. Good timing really. Being seen as a slut at the start of university was not a good look and set you up for the rest of your time there. So with my newly developed respect for myself, I wasn't really interested in getting together with anyone.

After a week or two, things levelled out and I tended to hang out most with the girls in Flats 18 and 23 and the guys in Flats 21 and 22. I was very careful not to be seen as one of the shaggers and that was the same for all of us really. Of course, it didn't stay like that for long, but interestingly there wasn't much bonking about. It was very much people getting into something more long term. It was almost as if starting university made us subconsciously seek out our first 'proper' relationships.

Mine was Ashley.

Ashley was in Flat 22, two floors below me. Ash could not have been more different to anyone I had ever found attractive previously. Tall, yes, but skinny. Perhaps a little bit camp. Think Jim Parsons from *The Big Bang Theory*.

We hung out in groups mainly, so I didn't notice the mutual attraction for a while – but something must have been there. The moment I noticed it was one Sunday afternoon in October. I was having an 'achieve nothing' day, sitting about, when someone rang the bell to the flat. I answered the door. Ash was standing there doing a sort of 'lean'. He asked me if I wanted to come down to their flat. It was all very innocent, but at some point – and honestly, I am not sure exactly when it happened – we got together. And bloody hell, did we get together.

We were both eighteen, attracted to each other, and had time on our hands. We shagged like rabbits.

It wasn't that long before we had moved his mattress up to my room and created a 'double bed' of our own. He brought up his little TV and video, and when we weren't bonking we were watching videos, generally touching each other, and being that sort of couple you hate to see when you are single and fed up.

My uni work didn't suffer from it. Luckily for me, my mate Helen was on the same course as me and lived in the flat below. She had a much better grasp of the basics than I did, which was a godsend for me. We were a good motivation for each other to get ourselves onto campus when we needed to be there and to do all-nighters in the computer room when deadlines loomed. I was (and always have been) pretty good at hitting deadlines and turning up to lectures and classes. Saying that, we might have turned up, but perhaps weren't the most dedicated. When we weren't making Kinder egg puzzles or I wasn't drawing willies on Helen's notebook, we were doing a fair amount of chit-chatting. I thought we hid it well until in our final year I found out that we were known by some on our course as 'the two blondes who sit at the back and chat'. To be honest, most of the lectures made sod-all sense to me and it was far easier to study for assignments using a combination of textbook cramming and asking Helen what the hell was going on.

More often than not, Ash and I would head to campus together regardless. I was a bit clingy. OK, very clingy. To be honest, when we weren't together I was probably talking about him. I seem to remember one whole bus journey from campus was spent demonstrating to a group of friends the face Ash made when he orgasmed.

Luckily for me, Ash was really clingy, too. It was most definitely a completely mutual thing. Come on, I had come from a girls' boarding school and suddenly I was at uni with a boyfriend, sex on tap, and absolutely no need to sit about waiting to get a phone call or letter from him. He was just 'there'.

We booked a trip to Europe together. Now that was incredible. New freedom, new boyfriend, new horizons. It was a weekend break that we spent a good portion of our student loans on with no regrets. Perhaps not traditionally romantic, but definitely an eventful three days. A waiter in a Greek restaurant refused to give us the bill unless I had sex with him. I stopped Ash from doing a cut-and-run as I reminded him that he wasn't telling his folks that he had spanked £400 on a weekend away with no travel insurance, and a call from a foreign prison might shatter the illusion of all work and no play. The second day consisted of me nearly shitting myself at the top of one of the tallest landmarks in Europe (It sways! The fucking thing sways!) and later taking photos of something we found on the pavement – we weren't sure whether it was poo or sick. It was later creatively named 'poo-sick'.

Poo-sick and sexual threats aside, it was a fab few days of bonking, cheese and weird continental beer that had a whisky top (?).

Ash and I were properly happy. I had my first Christmas exchanging gifts with a boyfriend. Our relationship had a real heady innocence about it. We were never apart. It wasn't long until we decided we were destined to be together for all time. On Valentine's Day the following year, we hopped on a train to the most romantic destination within our reach – the English Riviera. Over a drink in the most exclusive bar we could find (Wetherspoons) we decided to get engaged.

I can tell you now, there is nothing a father wants to hear more at his birthday celebrations than that his youngest daughter has just got engaged to some bloke she met at uni five months earlier. My brother was uncharacteristically sensitive, though, and did point out to my parents that it wasn't such a bad thing. It wasn't like I was injecting heroin and running off to Gretna Green with my dealer. I am not all that sure how that was going to make Mum and Dad feel any better, but I appreciated his support.

I think my brother knew that this is a thing that people often do when faced with their first flush of love and romance. He also was wise and knew that the likelihood was that we wouldn't last.

I have a theory that very few relationships that start when people are in their teens see out the long haul. Well, it's not so much a theory as something I have learnt over my years of observing relationships – my own included. Of course, this isn't the case for each and every person. One of my closest friends met her husband when they were in their teens and now, in their thirties, they are still as happy as they were then. Some people are lucky to meet their True Love at a very young age. The truth is that most of us suffer from First Love Blindness.

My innocent belief is that people go through a lot of personal growth in their twenties. I defy anyone to say that they are the same person when they are twenty as they are when they wake up, hung-over, the day after their thirtieth birthday. As I said, it can work for some young loves but these are incredible people who work very hard on their relationships, look after each other, and understand the process of give and take. My nineteen-year-old self was a bit too lazy for all that.

The months went on uneventfully. We planned to get married in the July after we finished university. We practically lived together anyway, but come our second year, we moved into a shared house together with a couple of other friends.

To be honest, it wasn't long into our second year that things started to fray at the edges a bit. Ash was great. He was loyal as ever. Maybe a bit too loyal. I couldn't go anywhere without him and it was starting to get a bit tedious. There were no girls' nights out with friends, no course mates' beers. Ash was always there. I did once try and sort out a girls' night when Helen's sister came to stay, but – no surprise – midway through the night he turned up at the same club with a couple of his mates. There was no escape. After a while, I started to feel suffocated.

I was starting to learn the first few hard lessons in love. The first one was something that I know many of you can relate to. When you are together 24/7 and you are both in the same candyfloss-tinted bubble of love, it's wonderful. You would walk around sharing a pair of trousers if you could, the desire to be together is so strong. The trouble is, the moment one of you starts to feel like it's getting a bit much is the moment the other person starts to appear a bit nuts.

Just before Christmas, I broke up with him. This was the second hard lesson. There are good ways to break up with people and crap ones. I am not talking about whether you do it face-to-face or via text, I am talking about how you deal with the actual break-up. Ash and I both fucked this up.

One evening we sat together and I explained how it couldn't go on as it was and that I wanted to break up. He cried. A lot. I cried. A lot. That night we lay in bed and held hands until we both fell asleep, snotty with tears.

You see, that was my first mistake. You either break up or you don't. I thought I was being kind, but I was probably making things far more difficult. None of which was helped by the fact that we still lived together and were going to have until at least May the next year. Five months to go through living together and being apart.

So – riddled with guilt and with the New Year celebrations on the horizon – I found myself standing next to an already wilting Christmas tree and asking him if we could get back together.

Oops.

The thing is, if you know in your heart that something is over, feeling guilty isn't going to magically get your heart to change its mind. I still knew it was over, but sort of thought that if I had another go, I could sort it out. It doesn't take a genius to work out that the best relationships are not founded on guilt.

New Year's Day soon came around. After realising the world had not imploded due to the millennium bug, I realised I needed to break up with Ash. I had started to hate it when he so much as touched me. It was all going through the motions and nothing more, but I was so worried about upsetting him and had absolutely no idea how to deal with it.

This time, when I told him it was over, he knew I really meant it. He did not deal with it particularly well. He knew he had no control of the situation, and his frustration came out as anger. Not in an abusive way, but it turned nasty very quickly. In hindsight, I know that it was all down to the fact that neither of us had any idea of how to deal with the break-up. We were both about to have a crash course in what not to do.

His room was upstairs and mine was downstairs, so that was some sort of help. I had a little lock on my door, which was a blessing, as Ash was fairly unpredictable in those first few weeks. Not that I was worried about my safety or anything – I just wanted to be left alone.

One weekend, I went to London to get a bit of space. When I got back, I couldn't get in. I knocked, hoping someone was about. Eventually, someone came and undid the chain. It was Ash. He stood at the door in front of me in just his pants with a bit of a semi. He told me that I had interrupted him shagging my mate upstairs and that he had better 'get back to it'.

It wasn't very nice. In fact, it was rank. Still, I was the one who had dumped him, so I had to suck it up. The good thing was that he was moving on and that gave me a bit of a green light to do the same.

Or so I thought.

After the intensity of the time I'd had with Ash, I wasn't that sure what I wanted. I needed a bit of a break from relationships. I wasn't giving up on the idea, but I needed a breather. My Love Soldiering could wait for a bit.

I was definitely in need of some nice times. Over the next few months, I enjoyed university life in the way that I should have done in that first year. Unfortunately, Ash was often lurking and ballsing things up for me. One particular time, I was getting close to an attractive chap from my course in a nightclub called Liquid. Just like a scene from Taxi Driver, Ash burst out of the shadows, Travis Bickle style, and threatened him. Looking back, I know now that he was hurting and felt out of control. After all that time together as a couple, seeing me with someone else must have been tough. He had thought that he and I were the real forever. I have no doubt that he would completely agree with me now that we were not, but at the time it took him a little longer than me to realise it.

Funnily enough, a week or two later I did hook up with said attractive chap from my course. We ended up back at mine. Things got hot and heavy by the electric fire. I knew at that point that I had definitely made the right choice in breaking up with Ash. Being with someone else didn't feel wrong in the slightest. Well, I say that. It did feel wrong when he proceeded to try and put his cock up my bottom. When I alerted him to the fact that he was about an inch away from the general lady-garden area, he claimed it was an accident. Intentional or not, it was a bit of a wake-up call. I was back in the unknown territory of sex and relationships with unfamiliar people.

There were a couple of other love interests between Ash and my next 'proper' boyfriend, but the only significant one was Marine Fred.

I have no regrets about any of my relationships, as they all taught me something, and I am definitely a better and stronger person for each and every experience. I will, however, say that I do sometimes wish I could go back in time to when I was 'seeing' Marine Fred and give myself a massive slap.

I met Fred at a uni night near the end of my second year. He was wearing nothing but a leopard-print skin – for absolutely no discernible reason. Fred was stocky, and my friends would probably pick him out of a line-up as being 'my type'. He wasn't afraid to act like a tit and was very burly. He was studying as a mature student. He was living in a shared house in the city until the end of term when he would be off to the sticks to live with his dad and work on a farm all summer with a couple of his mates. Before he left, we saw each other on and off. I was in the process of moving out of the house I was still sharing with Ash and into a house with a couple of friends. The university term was over and our liaisons were fairly casual. I had no reason to believe there was anything off about the situation. In fact, I was pretty taken with him. Admittedly, it felt a bit like I was putting most of the effort in – but after limpet Ash, I didn't mind. Plus, it was the best sex I had ever had. Ok, that isn't going to sound very fair on anyone prior to him, but the reality is that it had always been me who had put the work in sex-wise until I met Fred. He was the closest I had got with anyone to movie sex being a reality.

Ah, Fred. He also professed to be a real lover of giving oral sex. At that time, I thought it was massively unusual for a man to really love giving it, so I thought I had hit the bonking jackpot. Ash didn't like doing it, and I didn't know any different. In reality, most hetero males love giving it. Ok, not all are that great at it – but with a bit of enthusiasm and willingness to listen, most men can be pretty good at it.

After university life came to a close for the summer, I spent my time working at a local pub. You had to see my workplace to understand it. Words somehow just don't do it justice. They had a really strong group of regulars and, as rank as they could be, they were protective of me. I got used to them all and the regular requests to see my tits, but my friends took a bit more time to get used to it. One evening shift, my mate came along and propped up the bar near me while I worked. One of the regulars ordered his drinks, and I asked if he wanted anything else. His response was as follows:
'Yes. A tit-wank.'

The look on my friend's face stays with me.

I didn't yet drive, and regardless of the fifty-minute bus journey, I would get the bus out to the middle of nowhere once or twice a week after I'd finished work to meet Fred in his local with his friends. I say 'meet' him – most of the time I would meet his dad. Fred would turn up an hour or two later. Now, Fred's dad was a legend. I really liked him. In fact, I probably should've been dating Fred's dad. He told the most cracking anecdotes. My favourite was one about him getting pissed and taking a lady back to his hotel room, only to find out she had a penis. Well, maybe it was the way he told it – but trust me, it was brilliant.

I'd spend most of the night there and get the bus back to the city at sparrow's fart o'clock the next day. Not once did the git bother to come to me. Even when I had a house party for my birthday, the tubby bastard didn't bother driving down. He didn't even tell his friends that I was having a party. I remember so clearly their reaction when they found out:

'You had a house party? With drunk single girls? And we didn't get to go? Fred – what the fuck? You wanker!'

I wasn't all that innocent and/or stupid at the time. I knew that by not turning up to my birthday bash, Fred was not going to be a keeper. It was a truly random fun night with an 'eclectic' guest list. Presuming you all know that by the term 'eclectic', I mean really fucking random. Magically, somehow my friend Paul popped his head in. I had met Paul through a mutual friend, Big Bob (a whole story in himself that I will glide past). Paul was (and still is) one of the coolest men I have ever met. I had always had a bit of a thing for him and was thrilled that he'd popped along to my do. I was even more thrilled when we had a massive kiss before he left. Oh, I didn't mention earlier that for some reason I had decided to make myself a Union Jack dress for the party. Yep. Geri from the Spice Girls 1998 Brit Awards. A bit of an 'it's my party and I will randomly dress up as a nineties popstar if I want to'-type thing. Looking back on it, as we stood outside my shared house, kissing in the moonlight, to the untrained, inebriated eye it must've looked like Sting had finally copped off with Ginger Spice.

Anyway, back to Fred. What was his problem? Well, he wittered on a lot about being in some reality TV programme at the end of the summer and that he planned to defer his last year of university. In his head, he had got on it and was going to be off in August on his adventures, leaving me behind. But he didn't get to be on the show. He was stuck on a farm working all summer and was back at uni the next September.

But no, it wasn't just that. Nope. I don't remember how I found this out – I think he just told me at the start of the new term when he knew the game was up. Apparently, he had a girlfriend. Kim. Yes. I remember her name was Kim. She had left to go back home (wherever that was) at the end of the term, around the time that Fred met me. He thought he was buggering off around the world on a bus at the end of the summer, so he never worried about the possibility of either of us finding out. It didn't quite work out for him. He even told me that one morning when I was round at the house he shared in the city, Kim was due later that day. We were about fifteen minutes shy of bumping into each other.

I felt like such an idiot. In fact, a more accurate description would be to say that I suddenly felt like an overenthusiastic groupie to an out-of-shape nutter who would throw me a few affection scraps occasionally by putting his willy in me after a few pints. Oddly, his friends seemed quite unaware of Kim too, which softened the blow. They were still pissed at him for making them miss out on a house party full of pissed-up, single, twenty-year-old girls. I never quite had the heart to tell them that my party was, in fact, full of male uni friends and mildly racist regulars from the pub I worked in.

Drunk

Despite the brief bump to the start of the term over the whole 'Marine Fred/Kim debacle', my final year of university kicked off with a positive and perky vibe. I was finally out of the house I had to share with Ash and was living with two of my best friends. Best friends I still count on to this day. I know it sounds a bit wanky using the term 'best friends' as a thirty-five-year-old, but it's true.

I was single and happy. I had newfound friends and was (sort of) concentrating on my university work. I also had a weekend job in a bistro to keep the pennies ticking in.

One week in September, I got an invitation to Paul's house-warming party. As Alan Partridge would have said, 'Back of the net!'. I was so excited. Paul was just what I needed at that time. I would finally get a chance to hook up with a chap I'd had a little crush on for a while.

I arrived at his flat with my mate. Ok … it was immediately apparent that we were even more different than I'd first thought. His world was eighties punk goth. Mine was nineties Eurovision. It didn't matter. By the end of the evening, most people had left and we were having an old-fashioned canoodle on his living room floor. It was at this time that I noticed he did something hugely off-putting. He moaned when we kissed. Not full-on groaning – I mean like a 'mmmmmm' noise. I also remember him stroking the side of my body and softly stating that he had 'never been with anyone who had hips before'.

I still don't know what the fuck that meant.

Although we were seeing each other on and off for a few weeks, we never had sex. Whenever we were sort of about to, he would either do the moaning kissy noise or say something remarkably not sexy. For example, we were once sitting on my bed chatting when he told me about his vegetarianism. It was fine by me. I was a veggie at the time too, although I ate seafood as it was more of a dislike of meat than a principle thing for me. He was most definitely a vegetarian due to principles. I know this because as we lay there he told me that he used to eat fish, too, but that after a visit to the Sea Life centre he knew he couldn't. He had stroked a stingray and had realised at that moment that fish had feelings, too.

A few weeks into term, I was having a drink in the uni bar with a friend. There was nothing special about the day; it was late afternoon and we had just finished lectures for the day. In fact, it wasn't that often I went to the uni bar.

This particular friend, Ruby, was a bit of a naughty friend and we would have some good, silly fun. Sober or drunk, it was always silly fun. We were sitting near the pool table when this bloke bent right over the pool table in front of me to reach a shot. Ruby dared me to pinch his bum. So I did. He turned around. He was handsome and cheeky and took it as an opportunity to chat with us. He crouched down next to the table we were at and grinned. I was sort of seeing Paul, so was not all that interested. Ruby was attractive and outgoing, so my genuine assumption was that they were going to get chatting and 'get to know each other'. Although he was new to the university, he had changed his A-levels which had held him back a year, so he was around our age. We gave him some tips regarding events coming up. I headed off back home and didn't think anything more of it.

That Friday was the Hallowe'en fancy dress party at Time nightclub. Paul didn't fancy it. He was cool. I wasn't. Dressing up like a moron and heading to a shit nightclub was very low on the list of things he was up for. My friend and I were limited on fancy dress options, so went for 'murdered schoolgirls'. I know. It would now go against my anti-sexy fancy dress policy, but I was twenty at the time and was up for a miniskirt, tie and excess fake blood splatter.

Paul sweetly dropped Lisa and me off that night before he headed on to do whatever was more on his radar of appeal. We got inside, and it was the usual crowd – people we recognised from our courses and a general sense of familiarity. I felt a tap on my shoulder. It was that cheeky bloke from the uni bar. My heart did a little flip. This was not a good sign for Paul and me.

  Johnny and I were completely drawn to each other. I fancied him despite the fact that he was wearing a pair of white, slip-on shoes but was not in fancy dress. I quickly learnt that it was, in fact, me that he was interested in that day in the bar – not Ruby. Wow.

  He had the kind of charm that I imagine a spiv would've had during the war. You felt like he could have sorted anything out for you, and he had the knack of making me feel immediately that he was properly interested in me. We kissed that night. Yes. I am not proud of myself for that. I should have made sure that things between Paul and me were definitely closed before tonsil tennis with another chap, but there we are. Not that it excuses things, but the truth is, Paul and I hadn't even slept together. The chances of us lasting were about the same as those of Homer Simpson giving up donuts. But still, I shouldn't have done it. That night, Johnny took my number and we said our goodbyes.

  The very next day, I called Paul and broke things off properly. He was fine about it, and I remember him saying: 'well, we never really had a sexual relationship, did we?'. I didn't want to tell him that the reason for that was pure fear. If he moaned as we kissed, I wasn't sure that he wouldn't shout 'cowabunga' or similar when he ejaculated.

So there I was. I had broken things off with Paul and was now in the wilderness time of 'waiting for the call'. Now, please remember that these were the days of landlines. Yes, we had mobiles, but texting was very much in its infancy. I had to wait.

The call never came.

Well, I thought it never came. A few days later, my housemate found a 1571 message from him:
'Hi – it's Johnny from the other night. Just wanted to say hello.'

He had left a message exactly three days after we had met at the Hallowe'en party. He had also failed to include his phone number, so I couldn't call him back. Fuelled by frustration and enthusiasm, we even changed the outgoing answerphone message to include the line 'please leave your name and your number this time' in case he called again. Of course, he did.

It wasn't long before the cockney wide boy in the white, slip-on shoes revealed himself to be a locally born and bred student who still lived with his parents. This didn't result in any feelings of shattered illusions for me. I had no problem with the fact that he lived with his folks. If you'd seen the types of shit heaps some of the uni students I knew lived in, you'd understand. Some male students I knew would hardly take the dishes out of the sink before pissing in it. I figured that if he lived with his parents, he was less likely to introduce me to listeria.

I met his parents quite early on. When I say early on, I mean four weeks in. Man, was I brave. You see, I had never really been in the position of someone's parents having much of an influence on a relationship. To be honest, I always got on well with people's parents. I didn't really give it much thought. Whoops.

I was just about to join Johnny at his cricket club Christmas party. It was a smart affair with table service at a local Holiday Inn (not a cocktail sausage in sight), so I was in full frock-up mode. Johnny took me into his living room and introduced me to his mum. I stood there, all five foot nine of me plus heels, in a scooped-front, full-length backless number. In that moment, I saw pure fear and anger in his mother's eyes. She did not see an innocent, fun-loving twenty-year-old student. Nope. She saw a thirty-year-old woman who was about to abduct their fresh-out-of-school man-child for a night of vodka Martinis and light spanking.

You see, to make it much worse, Johnny had changed his A-levels and stayed back at school another year. Although he was only a few months younger than me, he was in his first year of university. Then there was me, in my final year, plus – let's face it – I had been around a bit. No, not so much in a slutty way (and, fair play, I had already had what I deemed to be 'serious' relationships), but in the sense that I had always seemed older than I was. By the age of fifteen, I had travelled across the world on my own. Johnny was the exact opposite. The most exotic thing he had done by that point was to have paella with his folks.

Needless to say, his parents could not have been more wrong about me. I was very much of a similar age to Johnny, and I had a relatively sensible head on my shoulders and could look after myself. However, I could also be a total tit.

The cricket club Christmas party was the first time in my life that I had been faced with a situation that gave me a sense of fear and nervousness similar to the feeling I would have in future years when I went on one of my internet dates with someone unfamiliar. Although I knew Johnny, I didn't know him that well, and I certainly didn't know any other sod there. Plus, there was booze available. Lots of booze. I would love to say that I behaved with discreet decorum. But I didn't. I would also love to say that this was the first and last time I would deal with any similar situation as badly. But it wasn't.

I was doing fine and had only had a few vinos – at least through dinner. Then the strap on my dress snapped.

Nothing fuels a feeling of 'pass me the wine' quicker than your boob popping out in front of a room full of middle-aged cricketers and their wives.

As it happened, everyone was very sweet, and one of the wives sewed me back in. That is one lesson I did learn. To this day, I always take a needle and thread with me in my handbag if I am in tricky clothing. Honestly, test me. Find me at a wedding or Christmas drinks, and I will have needle and thread in my bag.

So, fuelled partly by embarrassment and partly by the awards ceremony (have you ever been to a local cricket club awards evening?!), I drank a little quicker and a lot more enthusiastically. I held it together well. To be honest, had there not been a 'disco' afterwards, I may have been able to keep together a touch of class and a sprinkle of dignity.

And then it happened. The DJ went to make an announcement as I was walking past the dance floor on the way back from the toilet. For reasons completely unbeknown to me now – and probably not even then – I grabbed the microphone off him and, in front of everyone, made up a song on the spot that went something like:
'Everyone shooooould have paaants on their heeeead …'

The DJ took the microphone away, and – as if that wasn't enough for me – I promptly turned around, tripped over the leads to the speakers and fell quite literally flat on my face.

Johnny helped me up (thank goodness), and I did sober up a little at that point. I was very lucky that amongst all the commotion, my other strap didn't go and expose my second boob to anyone who didn't get to see the first one.

I woke up the next morning with no real idea of how I had got into my bed. I sat up and nudged Johnny, mumbling: 'Um. Sorry about last night.'

I wasn't sure what I was apologising for, but I had that hangover dread, and without any clue as to how we'd got home, I thought an apology was appropriate. I then noticed that next to my bed, next to our clothes (clearly thrown off with gay abandon the night before) there was a pile of coloured tablecloths. Johnny explained that as we were leaving he thought it would be a great idea to steal a load of tablecloths as they were his football club's colours.

And then it hit me. He was also a tit. I knew then and there that we were going to be happy together for a long time.

Technically, Johnny was my third 'proper' boyfriend, but in many ways, it was like being with my first. Jim and Ash were all dandy at the time, but it was with Johnny that I genuinely started learning about relationships on an equal plane.

I was Johnny's first long-term girlfriend. No surprises there. He was fresh out of school. I had already made some mistakes and was ready not to make them again. Or so I thought. After the intensity of Ash, I should have learnt that you didn't need to live in each other's pockets – but pretty quickly we were doing just that.

The biggest difference with this relationship was that it was very much founded on both sexual attraction and an actual friendship. It sounds unbelievably wanky to say this, but we were as compatible as non-sexual friends as we were as sexual partners. Our first official date wasn't the usual dinner and a fondle. Nope. It was a trip to the fireworks with Lisa. Yes, that's right. My mate actually joined us on our first date. Far from it being awkward, it was a mega-fun night, and as much as anything it showed that he got on well with my friends, which was a bonus.

Despite him being my third 'boyfriend', more and more we found ourselves learning and trying new things together. And I mean really trying new things. The way he looked up to me as the one who seemed to know what I was doing boosted my confidence. We found ourselves getting up to things neither of us had tried before. Some were innocent, some were not so innocent – but it was a great realisation for me that there are always opportunities to grow and learn in each relationship you have.

Along with some of the not-so-innocent experiments, there were the successful and the not-so-successful ones. Believe it or not, until I met Johnny, no one had ever made me orgasm. Yep. I was actually engaged to be married to a man who had never got me off. No wonder I called things off.

For the first time in my life, I was with someone who was cracking in the sack. I mean really good. He properly listened to what I needed and responded accordingly. Result.

As I said, some things were more successful than others. To this day, I still can't get my head around anal sex. If the idea of sexy time is having the sensation of what can only be described as a dagger being shoved up your bum, then fair play to you.

I was with Johnny when I bought my first vibrator. Wow – what a find! I was happy to have had a not-so-successful anal sex experience in return for one of those bad boys.

There were also the in-between experiences. Now, as bright and enthusiastic as Johnny was, he could also be a moron. One evening, he had the idea of sexy massage fun. Great! Fine with me. He'd brought some essential oils and got me to lie down on the floor. He got his hands to work. Christ on a bike, the smell was strong. Still, as I had only ever used baby oil and knowing I had a sense of smell similar to that of a Bloodhound, I thought all was well. After a few minutes, I agreed to swap over. Instead of waiting for me to get up, Johnny stood in front of me, bent over and pulled down his pants. His anus was not the view I was hoping for.

To make things worse, my back then started to get exceedingly hot. I got him to show me what he had been using. Oh shit. Pure essential oils. I had innocently assumed he had a mixer oil with them, but oh no – he had been rubbing lashings of pure essential oils into my naked back for ten minutes.

Now in those days, the bathroom was downstairs, and to get to it you had to run through the living room. My poor housemates had to suffer the sight of me running through to the shower, naked and smelling like an elderly prostitute. I got in the shower and the water just ran off my body. Well of course it did. I was covered in fucking oil.

I would say it was more common than not that our experiences would fail to go quite as planned. Our first weekend away in a hotel was a bit mixed. It started off beautifully. He put tea lights around the bath. We had wine. We got naked. Then I needed a poo. Yes, on our first romantic weekend away I had to get Johnny out of the bathroom as I had the shits.

Whether it was a good or a bad thing, it was the first time I could be with a boyfriend and not worry too much about them hearing me on the toilet. In fact, we were probably a bit too comfortable with each other. How many people can say that they have asked their boyfriend to check whether a tampon cord is visible because they're not sure whether they've put one in or not?

It wasn't always a bad sitcom. Sometimes things really worked out for us. He had a job in the summer doing odd jobs and managed to get me a job with him painting a flat. Not just any flat. It was the flat at the top of the building where his mum worked. The boss was sceptical about agreeing to it, picturing us just titting about as we were going out together. We really didn't. We worked hard and kept to schedule, finishing the painting even slightly earlier than expected. Pretty impressive. Even more impressive when you consider we would occasionally take time out to shag on the floor.

Of course, the inevitable was soon on the horizon. I was going to graduate and be off into the real world, leaving Johnny back plodding along at university. He had two years to go, after all. Now Johnny was a 'fly by the seat of his pants' type and was scraping by on his course. Not because he wasn't capable, but because he just wasn't truly applying himself. I couldn't be blamed; I studied hard, as I was determined to get a decent result out of my degree. As I was in my final year, I couldn't afford to fuck it up.

I started my very first 'proper' job not long after graduating. Johnny was working part-time at the football club, and all was well with us. Soon, the start of his second year came round, and my working life had a good influence on him. He started to treat his university studying as a full-time job. His folks were as sceptical about me as ever, but I knew I was a good influence on him.

The trouble was, all this 'good influence' crap wasn't much of an aphrodisiac. Ever so slowly, I started to feel a little like I was looking after him more than the other way round – which, if I was honest with myself, was what I wanted and needed.

The trouble is, the moment you start to doubt a relationship, the feeling starts to spread. It was always something or nothing, but little things like his mum bugging him to clear up his room and clean the car started to get on my nerves. Not because of her, but because I agreed with her. You know, it's not sexy to be standing with someone getting told off by their mum for being naughty.

Then there were other little niggles. One evening I found my bracelet snapped in two in his desk drawer. It had been a gift from a friend for my twenty-first. He had broken it, but instead of telling me, he had hidden it. Honestly, it wasn't that I was worried he was 'hiding other things' from me or anything like that. It just seemed a bit too close to the actions of a teenage boy hiding something from their mum. And there it was. I was starting to feel a bit like his mum. Ugh.

The writing was now starting to be spread right across the wall for Johnny and his 'princess'. Whilst he was one of the kindest and most thoughtful people I had ever known, and we had made some (very) personal discoveries together, it just wasn't going to work.

You know how I ballsed things up when I split up with Ash? Well, I did so even more badly with this one. Perhaps the two break-ups would've been absolutely fine had those I was breaking up with been on the same page as me. But break-ups rarely play out like that. Even if you both know it isn't working and that you are on a one-way ticket to single-town and vodka-ville, there is always someone left with a little more feeling than the other. That's what makes 99% of break-ups a bit shit.

Truth be known, I had always been in very vague and inconsistent contact with Mick. Remember him? Yes, the Australian. As things were going down the loo with Johnny, I found myself wondering more and more whether what Mick had said was true: that if I wanted to see him again, I would.

The funny thing is, I don't remember how I broke things up with Johnny. This was part of the problem. I knew we weren't working out and that I wanted to get out of the cul-de-sac that we had created together. However, I didn't really want to let Johnny go. He had become good friends with my friends and I felt like we could still be friends, too. Reading this, you are probably thinking something along the lines of that I wanted to both have my cake and eat it, and you would be completely right. You can't have all the cake you want, eat it, avoid regular brushing and not have all your teeth fall out.

So we remained friends. Friends who were close enough that occasionally he would sleep over and stay in our living room. Friends who were so close that on one occasion I lay next to him and kissed him until the early hours. I was a bit of a shitty friend, as he still had feelings for me and I felt completely neutral and didn't consider how much of a headfuck I was being.

I was always completely honest with him. Perhaps a little too honest. I told him about the contact I was starting to have with Mick. Johnny, being Johnny, was supportive. He reasoned that if I was to go out with someone else, Mick was a good choice. It was potentially a whole new life for me, and he understood that. Because he was so sweet. I, on the other hand, wasn't particularly sweet. I wasn't doing anything to purposefully upset anyone, and I definitely wasn't intentionally being insensitive – but I was being a total penis.

I have made (and probably continue to make) some questionable choices in my life – but I was about to make a real cracker.

I was newly single and full of ambition, and even had a shiny new degree under my belt. Instead of concentrating on settling down in my adopted city and getting a full-time job on the back of my shiny new degree and work experience, I went down the road of hopping from temporary job to temporary job while developing a relationship with a man I had gone out with for a few weeks when I was seventeen. A man who was fifteen years older than me and who lived in Australia.

What could go wrong?

Mick and I were soon in contact with each other with alarming regularity. Remember, these are days before it was standard to have internet access at home. I had to make a two-mile trek to the library just to check my emails. It wasn't long before we were telephoning each other a few times a week. Not an easy thing to do when you are dealing with an eleven-hour time difference. I was either getting up ridiculously early or staying up into the night to speak to him. Not that it wasn't worth it. He had the sexiest voice I have ever known. A sort of softer, smoother Crocodile Dundee. Luckily, the comparison with Croc Dundee ended there. No

Sue Barker handbag-face for Mick. Just that same gravelly, slow, Antipodean accent. Nice.

Over a period of just a few short weeks, things gathered pace. We weren't just exchanging flirty emails and late-night breathy phone calls. Mick would also write me letters. Don't get me wrong: hearing those three little words 'you've got mail' was fabulous – but actually receiving a handwritten letter, bursting with thoughts and emotions, was off the romantic scale. He would write pages and pages and tell me his deepest thoughts, writing song lyrics and reminiscing about how he felt when he first met me. I was just as passionate as a recipient. If I was lucky enough to have a letter waiting for me after work, I would take it to my room, sit by the window and whimsically thumb through the pages, thinking about his hands on the paper and breath on the envelope. Brontë for the new millennium.

I know. I sound like such a bell-end. The thing is, in many ways, Mick was a bit of an exception to my rules when it came to my Love Soldiering. I had only ever spent time with him in fantasy situations. Let's face it – I was always going to rose-tint the hell out of him.

It wasn't just letters I received in the post. He would also send photos. No, I am not talking about pictures of him bending over or rubbing himself in margarine. He sent one or two of himself, but more poignantly he would send me pictures of his house. The house he helped to build. The house that he invited me to live in with him.

Yes, you read correctly. I was going to move to Australia to be with him. I thought at the time that it would be a cracking idea to give up my family, my friendships and my whole life to shack up with a guy I'd spent two weeks with three years ago. I know I sound like a mentalist, but at the time it made perfect sense. It all seemed like it was falling into place. The words he spoke to me beneath the moon in Cyprus – 'if you want to see me again, you will' – would occasionally ring around my head. I thought that somehow the stars had aligned just for us. He said goodbye to me as I headed off to university, only for us to meet again three years later, after my graduation, ready to continue the rest of our lives together.

Or something like that. I don't know. I wasn't getting a lot of sleep. If you remember, I was up all hours on the phone to bloody Australia.

It was far from being an empty promise to each other. In order for me to travel and stay in Australia, I needed money. Money that Mick was happy to temporarily transfer to my bank account. I was going to learn to drive while I was out there so that I could use his BMW to pootle about in, as he had access to cars through his job. Police cars, I guess.

After feeling like such a mum with Johnny, I was relishing the idea of being looked after. Mick was going to grab me to his bronzed bosom, and I was finally going to be the one being taken care of.

The trouble was that I didn't feel all that looked after. I have tried hard not to quote *Sex and the City*, but in this case, it's too appropriate to miss. One episode referred to a 'good on paper' guy. The type of chap who should be perfect but somehow something isn't quite sitting right. If I was being honest with myself, Mick was a 'good on paper' guy. The problem with those sorts of men is that the bits that are written on paper never take into account their day-to-day nuances. Or, to put it another way, they ignore the little things that get on your tits.

Mick wasn't that great at making time for us to speak on the phone. He started off well, but after only a few weeks, four times a week was down to just once or twice. This wouldn't have been such an issue, but when I asked him why he wasn't calling as often, he got really shirty. I got a long-winded email stating that after a long day at work he shouldn't be expected to get up early or stay up late to call me all the time. Which was funny – what the hell did he think I was doing? It just got me thinking. I was about to pack my bags, tie the hanky onto the end of the stick, and head off to the other side of the world. I was giving up everything. I couldn't even take all of my things with me. I was giving up friends, family, possessions and – above all – my independence. It wasn't like I could get a job out there. I would have to be at his house playing mums and dads while he was at work. He was expecting all of that from me, and yet he couldn't quite make time in his week to make a couple of phone calls without making me feel like he was doing me a favour. Yes, he had a picket fence around his house and an ice-maker in his fridge, but even those aren't replacements for companionship and Marmite.

Despite my reservations, I wasn't going to give up on the Mills & Boon happy ending in Melbourne quite yet. I reasoned that we were just getting to know each other – warts, bitching and all. It would be fine.

Don't get me wrong – despite the plans to emigrate, I wasn't a hermit. I had a decent (although temporary) job at the local hospital. I was living in a shared house with four other friends, so there was plenty to keep my idle drinking hands busy. One Friday evening after work, I bumped into a friend of Marine Fred's. Remember him? He had some awesome friends, so it was great to see this guy again. I took him up on his invitation to head to the pub. It was a lovely evening. Gin and tonic was my drink of choice that night. Now, even you know that I am a vino girl, so to this day I have no idea why I was on the gin that night. Not that it mattered. It was a nice, long drink for a summer evening. Hell, it was the Queen Mother's favourite tipple. What could go wrong?

Later on in the evening, we bumped into one of my housemates. She was off to a birthday party at a pub down the road. I wasn't ready to throw in the Friday fun day towel just yet. Spurred on by sixty-five double gin and tonics, I decided that the party sounded like a good idea.

One thing is certain: going to that party was a decision that was going to change me. Maybe not that night, maybe not in a few weeks – but it was the start of big changes and bigger decisions. I have a friend who has a real issue with those pictures they put on the news of the 'last seen moments' of someone before they are found dead. He always says that he wishes he could reach into the picture and tell them to call someone, or to just run. When I look back at pictures taken before that night, I want to have a quiet word with myself. Although knowing 'drunk me', I would have told me to sod off and gone anyway. The question is, if I could do a Cher (turn back time) and make the decision not to go to that party, would I?

I arrived and sat down with my housemate and her friends. All was well; there was nothing of any significance to report. To be honest, it was just a pub room with the tables pushed back. The room was mainly filled with academic types, teachers and postgraduates. There was a huge range of ages, which made a change. As I was not long out of university, I mainly hung around with people near to my own age. I had absolutely no intention of meeting anyone. I had one foot out of the door and on the way to Australia. The trouble is, life doesn't always quite pan out the way you expect.

No

There he was. Tall, dark, attractive and – thanks to four litres of gin and tonic – looking, to my eyes, like Mr Big from *Sex and the City*. I wanted to talk to him, so I wobbled over to the group of people he was chatting with. He could see I was a bit pissed and found me entertaining. We got talking. He was called Pete. He was almost comically charming. Maybe in a soberer light he might have bordered on smarmy, but I was pissed and completely charmed.

It was probably only around twenty minutes before last orders were called. I had been on the booze since 5pm. Pete asked me if I wanted to go back to his house for a drink. Well, I thought this was a marvellous idea. Who wouldn't think it was a great idea to jump into a taxi with a man who you have known for less time than it takes to cook oven chips?

We got chatting in the taxi and I felt totally at ease. Well, I did until we got to his house. The Mr Big image I had created over the previous half-hour was shattered when he let me into his shared student accommodation. I excused myself and went to his bathroom. I called Lisa. She was glad I wasn't dead. I mumbled something about meeting Mr Big and that I was at his house. She told me to sober up and come home. It was at that point that I did start to sober up. I was in a random mature student's manky shared house. Away from the softly lit bar and in his 'natural environment', he was less Mr Big and more Mr Medium at best. I didn't know where I was, and I suddenly felt very vulnerable and incredibly stupid.

It then gets a bit hazy.

I did get a taxi back home. But I took Pete with me. There is no excuse for it. I was being a big, stupid slag. I could tell you that we didn't sleep together, but to be honest, I am not all that sure what happened. I know that he stayed the night. I know that he borrowed my toothbrush in the morning. I know that he used my toothbrush. I know that it was seeing him confidently brushing his teeth, stark naked, using said dinosaur toothbrush was the moment I just wanted him to bugger off.

I was hung-over. I vowed to never ever go near gin again. In the harsh light of my hanging day, Pete looked like a forty-year-old student. Still attractive, but a bit old and a bit inappropriate for me. Not to mention the fact that I was supposed to be going to bloody Australia to start the next chapter of my life. Needless to say, I knew there and then that the one thing that my night with Pete signified was that I didn't want to go. I had to stay in Blighty. It was my home, and the only thing I had in Oz was Mick. When we spoke that weekend, he knew. We were both kidding ourselves. He was lonely and I was feeling a bit lost and at a loose end. Now we can all agree that 'being at a loose end' isn't the best reason to emigrate. Together, Mick and I agreed we should call it off.

As for Pete – well, I never exchanged numbers or email addresses with him. He never asked for mine and I wasn't all that interested. I was too confused by my own behaviour. And hung-over. Being the small world that it is, though, it wasn't long before I received an email from him. He found my old university email through the library and took a punt. It was a friendly enough email. He wanted to see me again. Why not? Mick and I were officially over and I was curious to see what this Pete chap was really all about. We decided on a date a couple of days later. He was going to pick me up and take me out to a pub.

That evening, I was sitting talking to my fellow housemates about my impending date. I was starting to have some serious stomach churns. It was odd, though. I didn't feel nervous. I just felt like I wasn't sure if this was a great idea. I put it down to the fact that I was still in a bit of a head-spin after deciding to stay and not get on the fun bus to

Melbourne. My friends told me about good dates they'd been on and tried to put my mind at ease. Ria said that as long as the guy didn't turn up wearing chinos, it would be ok. I took her chinos and raised her a white roll-neck. You know those white turtlenecks? Del Boy used to wear them with a gold chain or two. Ugh. I know 'you can't judge a book by its cover' and all that crap, but there is one thing I just can't get my head around, and that is white roll-necks. A man who wears those looks like he wouldn't hesitate to come on to his teenage daughter's friends. He would probably try and lure them to his Lexus with promises of a Bacardi Breezer and a packet of Frazzles. He's the kind of chap who would still use the phrase 'afternoon delight' with absolutely no sense of irony when referring to sex in the afternoon. Yep. You know the sort.

The doorbell rang, and Ria went to answer it. After a minute or two, she hurriedly came back into the kitchen. She was almost purple from trying to stifle her laughter. A few seconds later, Pete sauntered in. He was cool. He was calm. He was wearing a white roll-neck.

Yes, my immediate reaction wasn't that fair. I did my best. I didn't laugh in his face. I kept myself collected, opened the fridge, and hid my face as I let out what I can only describe as a 'guffaw'. The next ten minutes were taken up by Sandy, Ria and me making up some preposterous story about Ria trying to put her keys in the toaster and thus making us all fall about laughing. How hilarious. Hmm. Anyway, against my roll-neck-influenced judgement, I still went with him on that date. It would be fine, I thought. It was just a drink.

 Once we got to the pub, he offered to get me a drink. I sat down. I suddenly felt overwhelmingly uncomfortable. I have no idea why – there was absolutely no explanation for me feeling like that. I just suddenly really wanted to go home. This was probably not helped by the fact that his drink of choice was called 'Old Peculier'.

 I didn't say anything and let him chat away. He was studying for a PhD and was aiming to be a lecturer at the university when he completed it. He was already teaching part-time as an associate tutor. He had a job and a life goal. It helped, as until that point I just thought he was one of those 'forever students' who refused to live in the real world and get a job. Those kinds of people are fine if they are from a rich background, but without the readies to back up that sort of lifestyle, you look like a bit of a tosser.

 I didn't feel myself relax at all that night. I felt out of my depth and just wanted to be in the cocoon of my little room. Just me, my duvet and maybe Now magazine. I said I was tired and wanted to go home. He finished his questionable drink of choice and said he would take me home. Before long, we were hurtling down the outer ring road, which was the wrong route completely. Just to add to the overwhelming sense of unease, it started to rain. Thick sheets of heavy rain lashed against the windscreen. It was dark, and as I was born without a sense of direction, I was completely disoriented. He went to take the turning to take me back home but turned too early, mistaking a lay-by for the exit. His car came to a standstill. The rain continued to thrash against the windows. My heart was beating so fast that I swear you could have seen it pounding through my top. Now, words like 'terrified' get bandied about a fair bit to refer to situations when people are in fact just a bit unnerved. In the same way, people use the word 'starving' when in fact they have plenty of fat reserves and are just being overdramatic to justify eating another Go Ahead bar. Trust me. I was terrified.

After what seemed like hours – but was in fact probably just a second or two – Pete burst out laughing. 'Whoops – haha!' He was completely embarrassed. I felt a warm vibe and I broke into a smile. He was not going to stab me in the face. He had just taken a wrong turning. He apologised, indicated right and pulled out of the lay-by. Phew.

He dropped me at home and I almost fell over myself getting to the door. There was no heady romantic, sober kissing that night. I just wanted him to sod off so that I could get into the house, take my bra off and chat it over with my housemates. That was the end of Pete and me.

Or so I thought.

I had no choice but to really start to think about my future. As I was definitely no longer running off to the other side of the world, I had to think about what I was going to do. I wanted to be a wedding co-ordinator. Two of my closest friends from school asked me if I would like to get a flat with them in London. It sounded perfect. London was where all of the opportunities were for what I wanted to do, and my mates would make the perfect housemates. We made a plan for me to move down when my contract was up on my room. My new future was set. I had three months to find a job in London ready for the move to the Big Smoke.

However, the contact with Pete didn't dry up completely. I received texts and an email. At work later that week, I was chatting with Mel about him. I was laughing about the roll-neck and the lay-by and the hopeful emails. Mel laughed with me, but then said something that I was not expecting at all:

'You like him, though, don't you?'

Oh crikey, no! No, no, no. I was one hundred percent not interested in seeing Pete again. Mel was completely unconvinced. She genuinely believed that this little chapter in my life was not quite over yet. I had no idea what she was banging on about. The idea of encouraging a relationship with a man who was just about old enough to be my dad and who had a minor BO problem was ridiculous.

But she was right. I did see him again. I have absolutely no idea why, but I agreed to another date. Perhaps if he hadn't had the option to email me and he couldn't have sent me text messages – if it had just been landline calls – then maybe I wouldn't have seen him again. What can I say? He slowly wore me down and I found myself agreeing to see him again.

This time, it felt better. He smelt better, for a start. Plus, there was not a hint of eighties clothing in sight. He was charming. So very, very charming. He made me feel beautiful just by the way he looked at me. He took me to Pizza Express. After dating fellow students, it was so fab to be with someone who had the money to take me out without the prerequisite wallet comparisons to check to see who could afford what. Ok, to some, Pizza Express wasn't anything special – but to me, anything that wasn't a Wetherspoons was a step up. I'm not joking. One friend of mine was taken out to dinner while she was at university by a fellow student. We thought it sounded terribly la-di-da. She later admitted that she had found herself at the bar in

Wetherspoons being handed the two-for-£5.99 menu and being told she could have 'anything she wanted off that'. Romantic.

It felt amazing to sit there with a man who was turning out to be very well read, who was a seasoned traveller, and who had a solid future with a decent job all ready and prepared for him to take. I didn't feel like I would have to do all the bum-wiping in the relationship – in stark contrast to how I had started to feel with Johnny. It felt like he would take control and look after little old me. That's what I wanted. To feel loved and to feel looked after.

It wasn't long before we started to see each other fairly regularly. He would bring me little gifts: ice cream, magazines. He would make me laugh. As he was studying, some days he was able to come and see me at work for lunch. I remember going back to his house one lunchtime and looking up rude words in his dictionary of slang. I remember that my favourite was something like:

'Cunty McCunt Lips: A term of address, using generic Scottish name. Often deprecatory, and occasionally used affectionately.'

Oh, the japes.

Although we had been seeing each other for a few weeks, we very rarely went to his house. My shared house was warm and full of friendships, and there was always something going on. His was cold and dark and didn't really have a proper sofa. I do like a sofa. One evening, we did pop round to his. We had grabbed a takeaway and ate it sitting on the 'not quite a sofa' sofa. We had some tunes on, which was cosy. It def made a change from *Coronation Street* and watching *The Best Little Whorehouse in Texas* for the sixty-fourth time. (Not that I minded. Awesome film. Brilliant.) I remembered I had some CDs in my bag, one of which was a home-made 'mix CD'. Yes, it's old hat now, but at the time the concept of 'burning CDs' sounded more like something I might do when drunk involving a CD, a toaster and a 'good idea'. This CD was one that Johnny had done for me. It was awesome as it had a load of songs on it that I didn't have and that we had found on some now-shut-down music file-sharing website. Things like 'Where Do You Go To My Lovely' and 'Say Hello, Wave Goodbye'. Eclectic. I popped it on and he asked where I had got it. I told him that it was one Johnny had recorded for me. He asked who Johnny was and I told him. We were still friends. I didn't think anything of it. Pete, on the other hand, did.

The only way I can describe it is like when you are sitting watching TV and suddenly all the power goes out. It comes out of nowhere and makes you jump. He went bonkers. 'How dare you come into my home with CDs of love songs from your ex-boyfriends?!' he exploded at me. He shouted and shouted. I felt dreadful. He was totally right. I mean – I knew that things were nothing except platonic between me and Johnny, but he didn't know that. Johnny was, after all, an ex-boyfriend, so I understood how Pete might have been angry. I understood, but at the same time I thought it was a bit harsh. He shouted some more and stood up, pointing at me, pointing at the CD. Tears just fell from my eyes and squashed into the brown patterned carpet. I tried to apologise and explain, but he was impervious to my words. He eventually stopped and went upstairs, leaving me on my own in his living room. I didn't follow him. I called a taxi and took my CD out of the machine. After so much noise from Pete, the house felt deathly silent and very hostile. Thankfully, soon enough headlights flicked past across the curtains. I let myself out and headed back home. I felt guilty, scared and incredibly confused.

I didn't hear from him that evening. I didn't hear from him the next day. It was around three days later that I finally got a text from him. I felt an overwhelming sense of relief. He had finally forgiven me. The idea that I could have hurt him so much that he couldn't even talk to me for so long showed just how much damage I had done. It was a bit dramatic, and I certainly couldn't have kept up that level of silence if it had been the other way round – but we were in a new relationship and had to learn about each other's insecurities and nuances. So far, so normal.

It would probably not be a huge surprise if I told you that Pete was intense. Being intense isn't necessarily a bad thing. I don't remember the first time he told me that he loved me, but I know I felt that he did very early on. I know that sounds wanky at best, psychotic at worst – but it is true. He could make me know that he loved me by the way he looked at me.

Pete got on well with my other housemates. No mean feat as – let's face it – he was eighteen years everyone's senior. One evening, a few of us were trying to play Trivial Pursuit. I was more interested in repeatedly playing my new Shakira single which frustrated Pete. When he went off to the loo, we gave him all the winning wedges so that the game could be over, he would be happy and I could get on with shoving popcorn down Lisa's bra. He took it all in good humour, and I started to wonder that maybe I had just mistaken maturity for intensity. Don't get me wrong, though. He had his moments. Later that night, my brother phoned me. As I was chatting with him, Pete shouted out, 'Your sister's knobbing a forty-year-old!', which my brother thought was fucking hilarious. I was a bit mortified. In fairness, it was quite funny.

As relaxed as Pete could be, I had to be careful. He was a bit sensitive. Pete's reaction to Johnny's CD was not a completely isolated incident. I didn't particularly like the way he could turn so quickly from everything being roses and unicorn farts to ignoring me for days, but I got fairly used to it. It didn't happen that often, and I started to learn what the triggers were and to be a bit more careful. I didn't mention ex-boyfriends at all. Full stop. I understood that. I didn't particularly want to hear about all of his exes. I just had to come to understand how his mind worked. It wasn't always easy, but he always made up for it when he was on good form.

I was always an open book with Pete. I have never been one for keeping secrets from people, and Pete was no exception. He knew from the start that I would be moving to London. It was something that didn't seem to faze him. As we had only been seeing each other a few weeks, I didn't consider any implications with regard to us – whatever 'us' was. I felt pretty sure that he loved me, but I wasn't all that sure about how I felt about him. I couldn't work out if his intensity was a good thing and down to his maturity, or whether it was actually a bit weird and perhaps down to an immaturity. I could never quite work out if he had an absolute handle on his feelings or absolutely no clue what to do with them. Essentially, I found myself wondering: was he a good guy or was he essentially just a bit of a twat?

With the London move very much still on the cards, quite rightly Nicole thought we needed to all meet up to have a chat about where we might live and general logistics. I arranged to head down on the train that weekend to stay with Nicole. We would meet Bella in the pub, have a few vinos, and go through the options. I don't quite remember actually inviting Pete, but he said he fancied a trip to London and I found him tagging along. I was a bit apprehensive. It would be our first trip away together. Up until then, if he was in a mood with me, he would just head off home. As we were both staying away, he wouldn't have the opportunity. I wasn't too worried. He could be a bit shirty with me, but he never revealed his bad moods in front of my friends. My housemates had no idea how shitty he could be. This was great because I never had to explain him to anyone. I knew how he could be. I could deal with it. We weren't betrothed or anything. It was no big deal.

I could tell on impact that Nicole wasn't all that sure about Pete. I put it down to the fact that he hadn't been invited. I didn't blame her. I looked a bit of a muppet, turning up with a 'boyfriend'. Bella arrived, and thankfully Pete soon made his excuses and left us to it so that we could talk about what we needed to talk about and get things sorted. Or so I thought.

The three of us started to go through dates and options. All fairly innocuous. We hadn't seen each other for a while, so it was mega to catch up. After an hour or so, Pete came back in clutching free papers. Papers with accommodation details in. He had decided to move to London. It was like a flicked switch. Suddenly he had decided to move to London and I was going to live with him. None of it made sense. I told him that I couldn't and that I was moving in with Nicole and Bella. Nicole asked him what was going on. Casually, as if he was repeating himself, he said he was looking for properties for me and him. Nicole was hurt as she thought I had been planning it with him all along and just humouring them. I was baffled. I knew it was a misunderstanding. I knew it would all be ok. Um. Not really. Pete decided to choose this moment to show people what he could be like. He went bat-shit crazy. What on Earth he thought I was doing there meeting Nicole and Bella for, I have no idea. The fact is, his perspective was that I had gone behind his back and that he was being abandoned for a big move to London without him. Had he not been shouting so much, it would have been pretty funny. As we were both staying with Nicole that night, I knew that he couldn't stay in this mood all evening. He stormed off. We stayed in the pub.

I apologised. I was confused. Nicole suggested we went back to her house. We got up and Pete came back in. Knowing he didn't have anywhere to go, he followed us. He said nothing. Nicole and I chatted as we walked. Uncertainty hung heavily in the air behind us. On the Tube, he was still quiet. Then it changed. We got off the Tube and started to walk towards Nicole's house. Pete found his voice again:
'You fucking cunt!' he shouted.

    The tirade continued. I didn't know how to handle it. By the time we got to Nicole's, he had finally shut up. Nicole showed us where we were sleeping. I thanked her and she left us to it. We went to bed in silence. He now wasn't talking to me. It was a bit of a relief. He fell asleep and I lay staring at the ceiling. Ever since we had met, he'd always known I was moving to London. I wondered if I had ever even implied that we would live together. I really hadn't. I was moving to London and would be living with Nicole and Bella. That had always been the plan. Pete had never suggested that he would even consider moving to London, let alone that he would move there and that we would live together. I didn't understand. We had only been seeing each other for a handful of weeks, and for half of those he had been in a mood with me. As much as anything, I was mortified. I was so embarrassed that friends so close to me had seen how he spoke to me. I wasn't sure if I deserved it or not. I'd never been called a 'cunt' by someone who'd genuinely meant it. Honestly, it's an experience.

I didn't sleep. Pete snored heavily next to me. I just lay there, waiting for daylight. Daylight finally came and I got up and got dressed. Pete woke up. I almost literally held my breath. I had no idea what to expect. He spoke. He was fine. Did last night actually happen? We left Nicole's house before she woke up. I couldn't face seeing her. I felt overwhelmingly guilty for all of the upset I had caused. I was grateful that Pete had forgiven me, or had at least let it go. The situation wasn't rectified, but I was glad he wasn't going bonkers at me anymore. One thing was for certain: I was desperate to get back to my own little bed in my own little space. On my own.

Pete was sorry. Very sorry. He said that we should have talked about it before going to London. I still didn't understand. What were we supposed to be talking about? He said we should have talked about the logistics of him also moving to London. He had assumed I knew that he wanted to come with me and that we would be living together. He genuinely thought that it was what we both wanted.

It was all a bit weird.

I needed to think fast. I was starting to confuse myself. I hadn't started to look for a job in London yet, let alone apply for anything – so who knows how I thought I was going to have the means to make such a big move? I had no idea who I was supposed to be living with even if I did go. I didn't want to live with Pete but I didn't believe that living with Nicole and Bella was an option anymore. If I moved in with them, my relationship with Pete might be over. Plus, after what had happened when I went to visit, I didn't think they would want anything to do with me and I didn't blame them. I had started to make a massive balls-up of things.

Wherever I was going to live and whoever I was going to live with, I ploughed on and started to look for a permanent job. Completely by chance, I came across a job advertised with a one-stop wedding shop – everything you need for a wedding in one place. As a budding wedding co-ordinator, I thought it was spot on. I wrote a detailed and passionate application and sent it off.

I only had to wait a few days before I received a response. It was a beautifully personal letter inviting me to an interview a few days later. I was so excited and also really flattered. They said that my enthusiasm leapt off the page and they wanted to meet me. I told Pete and he was really supportive. Despite some of his more unpredictable behaviour, when he was on my side he couldn't be warmer. He could look into my eyes and make me feel like it was all going to be ok, and that if I just said the word, he would run with me to the ends of the Earth. It's a hard thing to describe, but those moments of security could make all of my worries and concerns melt away and I could trust him all over again.

The day of the interview soon came. I suited up and headed to London. If I was being honest, the set-up at the wedding shop was a bit fur coat and no knickers. It looked chic from the outside, but when I started to look a little closer at the dresses on the mannequins, I noticed poor finishing and grubby hemlines. Something didn't quite fit. The employees were so warm and welcoming, but the office that I had my interview in was nothing more than a glorified stockroom. They were very sweet about my application and covering letter and seemed genuinely impressed by my enthusiasm. The job seemed straightforward, if a little commission-reliant.

On the train home, I thought about the wedding shop. What on Earth would I do if they offered me the job? Something about the place just didn't quite sit right. A bit like when you are talking to someone you know is talking bollocks. There was something behind the eyes of the people I met who worked there that told me they were keeping something from me. I kept thinking back to the dirty black hem on the full princess skirt at the bottom of the wedding dress in the centre of their entrance. Maybe it was just being on my own with my thoughts on that train, but something prompted me to think about what sort of relationship I actually had with Pete. Was there something behind my eyes when people asked me how things were between us? Was there something behind my eyes when a friend asked me if I was happy? Did my uncertainty show though my smiley 'yes' reply? Was the wedding shop the personification of the relationship I had with Pete? Were we all fur coat and no knickers, too?

My thoughts, however, were fleeting. Pete met me at the station. His smile and arms drew me back in. What on Earth had I been thinking? He really loved me. He made me feel safe.

The next day, I got a call offering me the job. I was at a crossroads. A full-on mega-decision-making moment. Should I take the job and move to London? If I did, should I move in with Pete or try to salvage the situation with Nicole and Bella? Or should I decline the offer and look for a job where I was? If I decided to stay, would I be staying to be with Pete? Did I want to live with Pete at all?

Everything churned around in my head, which soon began to feel like a cement mixer. In fact, my stomach felt as if I had just had a few cement mixer cocktails.[3] Something

---

[3] Cement mixer cocktail: hold one shot of Baileys in mouth and take one shot of lime juice. Mix rapidly in mouth by shaking head vigorously, then swallow. Or put Baileys into a shot glass until about two-thirds full. Top up shot glass with lemon or lime juice. Drink shot. No, I'm not kidding. It's a real thing.

about the job at the wedding shop didn't sit very well. I knew I had to turn it down. I wasn't all that sure anymore that I wanted to move to London at all. I spoke to Nicole. She was so good about it – any reservations she had, she hid well. I plucked up the courage to tell Pete. He didn't bat an eyelid. I was beginning to realise that although I had known him for a couple of months now, I still didn't really know him at all. I thought he might have had something to say about me turning the job down, but he really didn't. Perhaps he was happy where he was and happy with me. Who was I to argue with that? One thing I did have to face was that I was soon to be looking for a place to stay. So was Pete.

As luck would have it, my mate's partner was also looking for somewhere to stay and someone to share with. I considered it for about six seconds and agreed to hop on the rental train with her. I just had to find some sort of way to tell Pete. I assumed that as he wanted to live with me in London, he would have wanted to live with me here. Um, actually, he didn't. He had already applied for a place in halls. I was free to move in with Lily. Phew. If I was honest with myself, I felt like I had dodged a teeny tiny bullet.

I was sad to say goodbye to the big, shared house, the place from which I had nearly packed up to head to Melbourne. I was now packing up for climes a little closer to home – three streets away, to be exact. Pete helped us both move in, and in those first few days, there was no drama. Lily was into a bit of TV karaoke[4] and we both loved *Sabrina the Teenage Witch*. Highbrow. Things skipped along nicely for me and Lily. For about five minutes.

Now, for those of you who have been in a relationship with someone who is, um, a bit unpredictable (yes, let's go with unpredictable) you know how you deal with them. In your own little bubble, things can be justified and behaviours can be masked. But when you are enclosed in a small place – for example, a two-bedroomed flat – with a third person, it's a little bit hard to disguise things. Once you've got someone else who comes in from the sidelines to the inner circle, it's hard to ignore. With a little bit of hindsight, I can now see that there was a large shit about to head for an inevitable fan.

I knew Pete was not the most laid-back person in the world. I knew that I was not someone you could describe as 'easy-going'. We were like a freshly shaken salad dressing – the balsamic and olive oil never quite creating a proper solution but always hanging in the balance. Sometimes the vinegar would settle on the top; at other times the bubbles would appear. Although I was still with him, I didn't see him as my True Love at that point. I had started to realise that

---

[4] Pretending your remote control is a microphone and singing along to "Magic".

perhaps love wasn't the thunderbolt, musical extravaganza I had thought I might find. In fact, it was quite different. I had heard many times about how relationships had to be worked on in order to succeed. I could see now that the truest love was something that had to be worked upon.

 And work on it I did. Despite having the tendency to be highly strung, I found myself more and more looking for the easy route to please him. I couldn't be selfish about it. Relationships were about giving. I had to learn how to be in one. This wasn't university-style young love anymore. This was the real world. I was learning. I was twenty-two and had only ever had relatively juvenile relationships. I was now seeing someone eighteen years my senior. I was playing with the big boys now. I had to step up.

 I soon realised that if I tried to disagree with Pete, it made him unhappy. The moment he wasn't happy, he would fly off the handle, and then more often than not I wouldn't see him for days. Those silent days always filled me with worry and regret. It was always my fault. Something I shouldn't have said. Something I shouldn't have done. I was forever trying to please him, never quite knowing where I was going wrong.

 I can't say that it didn't take its toll on me. Here's a little fun fact: I used to bleed when I pooed. I know. Sexy. I know now that I suffered from ulcerative colitis. I kept my symptoms to myself. Nothing brings all the boys to the yard more than bowel disease. I spent half my time on the loo in those first few weeks with Pete.

So, you are probably wondering what my bowel movements have got to do with any of this. Well, I hadn't been too well. Anyone who takes medication will tell you that if you are spending a red circle print amount of time on the toilet each day, then there is a chance that any meds you are taking won't be all that effective; they'll most likely be going straight through you. Now, I wasn't on any colitis meds at the time – I hadn't been diagnosed at that point. I had only one long-term medicinal commitment. The Pill.

Now, as stupid as I sound, I wasn't that bad. I knew I hadn't been too great health-wise, but trying to not have sex with Pete wasn't an option. I wanted to make him happy. He would occasionally drop hints that he found the students in his tutor group attractive. There was one girl he talked about quite a lot. He told me how she was into James Bond. One day I was wearing my (awesome) Bond Girl t-shirt, and he asked me if he could have it and give it to her. I said no. I wasn't quite that submissive. Still, it stuck in my head that I needed to stay on my toes. If I didn't make him happy, there were other, younger women out there who were ready and willing to do it for me.

One particular night, I felt a bit backed into a corner. I hadn't been too well but I didn't have the balls to ask him to use a condom. I know. I was fine with him putting his penis in my vagina, but God forbid I should pluck up the courage to ask him to put a mac on it. The next day, I went to the doctors and asked for the Morning-After Pill. See, I wasn't totally naive. Plus, I knew that as long as I took the Morning-After Pill within seventy-two hours, I would be covered. All fine. Pete was none the wiser. Everyone was happy.

And that would have been a great plan. Except for one thing. One terrifying fact. I swear that if they taught this in schools, there would be significantly fewer teenage pregnancies. Did you know that the statistics for the Morning-After Pill's success rate actually take into account all females having sex at any point in their menstrual cycle? Stay with me on this. I promise I have a point. The reality is that if you only take into account the females who are at that marvellous peak point in their menstrual cycle when they are ready to conceive, well then, in those women, this magic pill is only 60% effective.

Apparently, when I popped that pill, I was in that 40% minority.

I was twenty-two and pregnant. I hadn't quite seen that one coming.

Wrong

I saw my doctor. He was Dutch and fabulously laid-back. He instructed me to (adopt Dutch accent for this): 'Go talk to your friends, have some wine. You'll decide what's right for you.'

I didn't need to do that. I knew. Hell, this baby had survived the Pill and the Morning-After Pill. Who was I to stop it in its tracks now? I considered that having a baby together might be the glue to hold Pete and me together (HAHAHAHAHAHA). Saying that, I wasn't blind. I knew that things between us might not work out. I had to make the decision to go ahead with the pregnancy whether Pete was still going to be there or not. I had to be ok with being a single parent.

I took a deep breath and called Pete.

He was happy.

Phew.

I was going to have a baby.

Wow.

I told my boss. That was fun. I had been pregnant as long as I had been working there. Whoops. It meant I was only entitled to statutory maternity pay, which was a bummer. But apart from that, work things were straightforward. Pete stayed with me at the flat more and more often. He was still studying and doing his associate tutoring, so I didn't worry too much about money. I would get up and get the bus to the hospital. Pete would head out to the university or the gym. We had a little routine.

But it was a little routine that involved me being Suzy Homemaker. I was happy if I was making him happy. The pregnancy didn't stop his demands. Slowly – very slowly – he got a little bit worse. The turning point of realisation came when he arrived home from the gym one evening. I had just got home from work. He came in and sat down and asked me what my problem was. I had absolutely no idea what he was getting at. He stared at me. 'You haven't even bothered to ask me if I want a cup of tea,' he said. And that was it. He went apeshit. He went full-on bat-shit crazy and I didn't see him for three days.

I had absolutely no idea what had set him off that day. I didn't understand and had no idea how to deal with it. He just saw the red mist. Maybe I should have made sure he was comfortable when he arrived? I ran the events over and over in my mind. One thing I didn't bank on, though, was someone else being there. Lily was in the living room and saw the whole thing. She told me he was being a wanker.

To you, it might sound completely obvious, but to me, it was a bit of a revelation. He hadn't yet shown his mood swings to anyone else. Lily told me that she had heard other arguments and had been worried. She told me to be strong and that it wasn't my fault. Hearing that was like a big dose of Sudocrem on my emotional Chinese burns. Over the next three days, with Pete gone, Lily made me realise that things didn't have to be that way; that if he truly cared about me, he would put me first. It was just so nice to hear. I didn't quite believe her; I mean, love is about give and take, surely?

Pete came back a couple of days later. He said he was sorry and that he loved me. I melted back into him. He genuinely meant it. We were having a baby and he wasn't going to go anywhere. He even told me he would work on his temper, something that he hadn't even acknowledged he needed to do before then. It was brilliant. Lily had made me realise that his behaviour was shit. Pete had admitted he was out of order. It was all going to be fine.

Except it wasn't.

What started that day was a pattern. He would go bananas over nothing and leave me for a few days, often heading to Poole or France to see his family. A few days later, he would come back full of apologies and regret. His studying was on hold as he didn't have the money to pay the fees. This meant his tutoring dried up. I was working full-time. He was pottering full-time.

There were times when he went too far. He pushed me to the ground when I was around thirty weeks pregnant, leaving a bruise on my chest. The frustration that he couldn't get his point across eloquently enough got the better of him. It was an odd one. He was sorry but said the bruise must have come from somewhere else. The trouble is, once something like that has happened, you are always waiting for the next time. A bit like when your mum or dad would threaten to give you a smack. They just need to do it the once for you to know that they mean it when the threat comes. In fairness, physical expressions of frustration from Pete were few and far between. He was much more the seasoned professional when it came to words and silence. To be honest, whatever had happened, I knew it was always going to be my fault. So I gave up.

Although I had made the decision to have the baby whether Pete was around or not, the reality isn't quite so simple. I was terrified of doing it on my own. I had barely ever even held a baby, let alone known what to do with one. Pete was so confident. My family were understandably hugely sceptical of my situation. After a while, we had nothing to say to each other. It wasn't intentional. We just drifted apart. I became increasingly withdrawn. It was hard to see friends because I was never sure of what sort of mood Pete was going to be in. If I tried to meet up with anyone, he would tag along or go bananas.

Occasionally, I would have a little reality reminder. A little nod that my friends were still going to be waiting for me on the other side. It was always the simplest of things that made the difference. One lunchtime, Johnny came to see me at work. He brought me a jacket potato and I ate it in his car. For the first time in four months, I felt relaxed. We sat in the little cocoon of his Renault Clio. I rested my potato on my bump. We talked and laughed. I got indigestion. It was all so lovely and normal. I never told Pete.

The pregnancy progressed with no real issues. I love hearing about mums-to-be worrying about how much shellfish there is in a crab stick and whether the sherry in the trifle will give their unborn foetus abnormalities. I never had those sorts of worries. I was too busy wondering whether Pete was going to smack me round the head with a frying pan or just hug me and tell me everything was going to be fine. Or both.

I needed Pete near me. I was starting to feel increasingly insecure about coping on my own. When I found out I was pregnant, I was all Billy Big Balls about it. Oh yes. 'All the single ladies'. I can do this with or without Pete! But in the cold light of the heavily pregnant day, I wasn't so sure. Pete was so comforting. He knew what he was doing. Pete had no fears about being a dad. He seemed to absorb all my concerns and make them disappear. Unfortunately, he was still disappearing, too. I tried to understand why he would leave. Perhaps it was his way of diffusing the situation. It was extreme, but he was hot-headed and I could see that by walking away he was projecting his anger elsewhere. Although it also had the effect of confusing the shit out of me. He always left in anger and was always motivated by something he said I had done wrong. I wanted to be better. Each time he left I wanted him back. I wanted it all to be ok. I wanted him to know I was sorry. I wanted him not to be mad at me. When I was thirty-eight weeks pregnant, he had another 'moment'. I begged him to stay. Begged. I was terrified. He was going to leave me and I was going to be on my own. I would go into labour and I would be alone with a baby I had no idea how to look after or cope with. He left anyway. I didn't hear from him for three days.

 We had no money. He had no earnings. He didn't even sign on. We had my wage and just about survived on that. His flouncing-off trips were funded by a credit card I had no access to. Thankfully, the credit card wasn't in my name. I told my boss that I wouldn't be returning after I had had the baby. I don't really know why. As I wasn't in receipt of maternity pay from them, I didn't see the benefit in staying.

The big, looming issue was that we were going to have to find somewhere else to live. Lily was endlessly supportive of me, but she couldn't live like that. More to the point, the landlord didn't want me in the flat if I was going to be nesting a newborn in the en suite. As vulnerable as I was, I still wasn't sure about living with Pete. He would still periodically leave me. I didn't know if I was coming or going. Fucking hell. How had I got into this position? I had just wanted to find a nice chap and fall in love. Not one bugger warned me how hard it was going to be. I hadn't realised that if someone loved you, then you owed them. That they'd offer you their heart and then you have to give up a piece of yourself. I didn't remember it being like that in any romantic fairy tale I had ever heard. Saying that, you never do get to see what happens 'ever after'.

I didn't go into labour with Jessica on my due date. I think she quite rightly wanted to stay put. She was two weeks overdue and took three days and two epidurals to come out. People say that when your baby is finally born, you have an overwhelming sense of love and peace. It wasn't quite like that for me. Pete was there during the early part of the labour but left fairly quickly. After seventy hours of prodding and pushing, I was all alone in the delivery suite. The effects of the second epidural had faded enough for me to get up. I swung my legs off the bed and looked at the wrinkly thing in the wheelie cot. It had a little hand-knitted pink hat on. It was sleeping. I then caught sight of myself in a long mirror. I stood up and turned towards it. My white nightgown was almost completely saturated with blood. I gingerly took it off. I looked and felt like I had just survived a car accident in which my vagina had taken all of the impact. I stared at the reflection in front of me. The saggy, empty belly. The engorged boobs. The crusted blood all over the torso. I turned again and looked at the cot. A baby. My baby.

What the fuck had I done?

That first night, I didn't sleep. Three nights in a row of no sleep. I had a whole other person to look after. I had a daughter. I was a mummy. I was in pain and suffering from exhaustion. Still, I had no choice but to buck up.

I hardly remember the first couple of weeks. I don't remember talking. I know I must have done, but I don't remember uttering a word. I plodded around in a dreamlike state, hanging onto the edges of reality. Despite not working, Pete didn't get up to Jessica in the night. I hardly ever slept. I gradually started to care less and less about how I felt. I just wanted to be there for my little girl. I would have moments when I sincerely believed I could do it on my own. Those moments were always quashed by Pete. I'd be trying to soothe her and he would walk in, take her from me and calm her. He knew what he was doing and I didn't. It wasn't his fault; it was just the way it was.

I had been granted another month at the flat, but the sand was quickly passing through the egg timer. If I didn't act quickly, I was going to be left with nowhere to go. Pete had no money. The statutory maternity pay was hardly clearing our day-to-day bills. I had cut myself off from most of my family and friends. My parents were abroad. In just a few weeks, I was going to have nowhere to go.

Pete left me to it. He still had his room in halls. He was 'all right, Jack'. Believe it or not, he sodded off to see his family in Dorset. He just told me not to worry and to go and see the local council. So I did. One hot, muggy August day, still bleeding from the birth, I walked to the doors of the council and took a ticket. The council office waiting room was heavy with despair. Everyone seemed to have a look of wretchedness. Some were just impatiently waiting to see someone about their council tax. Others were like me – sitting hopelessly, looking for a way out. Jess was fast asleep. I envied her pushchair. Man, I wanted to climb in there with her and just sleep. Two years earlier, I had been graduating. Two years earlier, I had been so full of optimism and excitement. Jess woke up and started to scream. I knew how she felt.

We got called to the counter and I explained why I needed to speak to someone. They asked me to take a seat again. A few moments later, I was ushered into a private room. I took a seat and gently rocked Jess's pushchair back and forth. A housing officer came in and introduced herself. She asked me to explain all of my circumstances. She was one of the kindest people I have ever spoken to. You know how it is when people are so nice to you that they make you cry? She was one of those. We went through the paperwork and she reassured me. She told me that being a single mum was the best thing that had ever happened to her. She reassured me that you get to make all of the decisions and never have to worry about whether someone else will be as committed as you. It made me feel better. I was sitting across from a confident single parent who was there to help me. With no family, no money and the end of a rental agreement, I didn't have many options. I was told I would hear from them soon with information as to how they might help me.

And she was right. Only a few days later, I received a letter in the post. I will never, ever forget reading those first few lines:

'Re: Application for Homelessness'

They had assessed me as homeless. Fuck.

It was a genuine mixture of fear, relief and shame. Things should have never got to this stage. Private school upbringing, university, loving family. Now homeless with a baby. It was ridiculous. Still, unless I was suddenly going to start being able to shit money, this was my situation and I had to deal with it. I now had to play the waiting game.

Sadly, the waiting game could not be played at the flat. I had to pack up and shove off. Pete put my things in storage and I headed off to my friend Bryony's house. Bryony helped me when I was at my lowest, and I will never forget her kindness. She offered me her living room to stay in for a few days. For those few days, I slept on her floor with Jess by my side. I pottered, cleaned and generally kept Jessica happy. I waited with optimism to get a peek at a rainbow of hope for our future.

I didn't wait long. After four days, I was offered the chance to move into a flat. I had no idea what to expect. It was a ground-floor maisonette. The area seemed quiet enough. The flat itself was a total shithole. Do you remember that fashion for 'rag-rolling'? Well, the previous tenant had. They had also used brown paint. It looked like they had left the flat after a dirty protest. There was an inch of what can only be described as scum all around the skirting. It was pure mank. Still, it was my mank. I was passionately grateful for the help. I would clean it up and it would be fine. Somewhere that Jess and I could call our little home. I would get my head together, and once Jess was a little older I would get a job and soon I would be back in the real world. Bosh.

The thing was, I didn't know if Pete and I were together or not. I guess you could say he was drifting. Despite my bravado, I was pretty scared when I was alone. Not because I didn't feel safe, but because I was terrified of not being a good mum and of accidentally dropping Jessica on her face or similar. Unbeknown to me at the time, these are standard mum worries. At least now Jessica was here, frosty relations with my family had thawed. My phenomenal sister came all the way to see me and even bought me a double bed.

I was the recipient of the most tremendous acts of kindness. One from a complete stranger. I had been in the flat for just a few short days when I came home to something hanging from my door handle. It was a bag brimming with baby clothes. Someone had seen me move in with a small baby and left me some clothes to help me out. Another time, in the dead of night, I heard a knock at the door. Pete had just left after going berserk about something or other. I opened the door to a neighbour who wanted to see if I was ok. They handed me their number on a piece of paper and urged me to contact them if I ever needed some help. You know, there are plenty of people out there who are incredibly shitty and judgemental about council estates, but I had never felt as looked after as when I moved into that council flat.

When he was in the right frame of mind, Pete would be there to help me. Without him, there is no way I could have managed to make that shit-den into a home. We were trying to make things work. I was trying to make things work. Sometimes it would be ok, and at other times it was awful. He would stay a few days and we would be an idyllic family unit. Then the red mist would come and he would leave me. It was like a record-breaking rendition of the hokey-bloody-cokey. He was forever putting his left leg in and then whipping it out again. Just to put it into context, Pete left me so often that my adjacent neighbour thought he was an airline pilot. I shit you not.

Believe me, I wanted things between Pete and me to work out. I tried everything. I did all of the night feeds, I cooked, I cleaned, I decorated. I had sex with him. I would do anything to keep him happy. Anything. In the times that he wasn't speaking to me, I wouldn't eat. I was desperate to be thinner. I would starve for days thinking that somehow being thin was the answer. Not a marvellous combination when you are up all night with a twelve-week-old. I was supposed to be on the Mini-Pill, but I didn't understand it. You have to take it at specific times or some bollocks. I wasn't listening to anyone, least of all my doctor's explanation of contraception. I had just had a baby and wasn't going to have another anytime soon, that was for sure.

The trouble is that when your body has just had a baby and you have all of the baby hormones still pumping through your blood, then all your body wants to do is be pregnant. You have to be so bloody careful. And I wasn't. One sad morning, I found myself slumped in a public toilet, weeing on a stick. Blue light flooded the cubicle. Jess slept in her buggy in front of me. I was pregnant again. Pregnant, and with a twelve-week-old baby already in tow. Do you think I genuinely wanted to be having sex? God, no. I didn't want underpants near me, let alone a penis, but I didn't know how else to keep Pete. And now I had paid the ultimate price.

Anyone who has ever been through the trauma of a termination will probably feel how I feel when I see them on TV. It all looks so fucking easy. Take a few pills. Job done. No. First, you have to wait. I had to wait three weeks, so I was seven weeks pregnant when it happened. Three weeks of being pregnant; three weeks of vomiting and exhaustion when you know you are waiting to do the unthinkable. Pete still expected everything that I had been offering: looking after Jess day and night, cooking and cleaning when he was there. Having sex.

I went in as an outpatient. Pete had Jess. I took a cocktail of pills and had to wait hours. I then had to take a second dose and wait for the expulsion. The sad thing is, as I lay in that hospital bed, I was grateful for the rest. I was completely exhausted. Emotionally, I was numb. Physically, I had hit my limit. I slept and slept. I was in a lot of pain, but I slept. They took me in for analysis. I was told they had seen that the foetus had been expelled. It is probably the single worst statement I have ever heard. I still didn't cry. I just didn't feel like it. I was offered an up-the-bum painkiller. Wow. Those things are astounding. If you're ever given the option of pain relief, then have one of those. Pete came to the ward with Jess but was asked to leave before I could see them. It would have been too upsetting for the other patients. I hobbled down to the waiting room. I remember so clearly seeing Jess. Her pink little cheeks. Her dungarees, with their little windmills sewn into the knees. She was smiling. At that moment, I felt my heart break in two.

Horrific as it was, I knew I had made the right choice. By the age of twenty-three, I had had two unplanned pregnancies. One I had kept, one I hadn't. As sick as it would always make me feel, in my heart I knew I had made the right choice for both. I also knew that I would never be quite the same again.

Now, we all know that I didn't stay with Pete. If I had've done, this would have been one piss-depressing story. The question is: how do you get out of that cycle? You know that I could go on about things that happened in the months afterwards. I will save you the anecdotes. None are particularly jolly. As an outsider looking in, it would have been easy to scream at me to stop the cycle. Pete turns up, Pete and I are happy, Pete, Jess and I are a happy family unit, I tread on eggshells, Pete gets pissed off, Pete goes bananas, Jess and I are left on our own, Pete disappears for days, Pete eventually turns up, Pete is sorry, I forgive him, Pete and I are happy, and so it continues.

You would think that perhaps it was the moment he had sex with me when I didn't want to that it would have been one step too far. No – I coped with that. I lay there with tears falling down the side of my face. I prayed he would finish and wouldn't notice my tears. I still saw it as him being happy and therefore us being happy. One of the final clinchers was when I was due to go and see my parents. They were living abroad and had paid for me and Jess to go and see them. On one of his good days, Pete had offered to take us to the airport. Fab, I thought. It wasn't one of my brighter ideas. He drove specifically to make us late. He was trying to make us miss our flight. It was awful. I was desperate to see my mum. No, I was desperate. I started to cry. Jess was next to Pete in the front in her car seat. I was sobbing in the back. Pete turned around and thumped me in the face. He said he did it so that I could 'pull myself together'. Well, it definitely shut me up.

By some miracle, we got to the terminal in time to get our flight. He said he was sorry but that he'd had to do it. I said nothing. I got Jess into her pushchair and grabbed our little suitcase and headed straight for check-in. I didn't look back.

The time away gave me the peace I needed. I could put up with a lot, but what I couldn't forgive was an attempt to keep me away from my mum. I needed my mum. I didn't tell her anything that had been going on. She knew I wasn't happy and that things weren't great, but I spared her the details.

I needed the perspective that the trip gave me. Away from everything, I was a better mum and a happier person. I started to believe that I might deserve better than all that I had been putting up with. I started to believe that Jess and I would be better with distance from Pete.

Getting back on that plane was one of the hardest things I had ever done. I knew that I would be better off away from Pete, but I didn't want Jess to be without a dad. I wasn't sure I could cope on my own. Was this my only chance at True Love? Was this the final hand I had been dealt when it came to my love search? Could I pick myself up out of the shit storm that was Pete and me? Could I head off into the sunset with Jess to make a better life? I wondered if I had already had all of my chances. I was a fool to have broken up with Ash, and with Johnny. I should have worked harder on what I had with them. I had taken the gamble. I had backed the lame horse.

My mum watched me and Jess disappear around the corner towards the security check-in. Only when I couldn't see her anymore did I let the tears fall. They poured, monsoon-like, down my face. Jess looked up from her pushchair and smiled. My heart ached for her. I felt a huge sense of impending doom.

Pete started to realise that I'd had enough. He could see that I was starting to slip away from him. Something had been triggered inside me that made me start to believe that I would be ok on my own with Jess. I didn't need him anymore. For the past couple of years, my life had been spent balancing on one massive eggshell. I had been trying not to smash it; trying not to fall off. Now I wanted to sit on the hard-boiled egg that was life on my own as a single mum.

A good friend offered me the chance to help out with her business. She ran a tutoring business and was looking for a manager. It was a total godsend. My maternity pay period had come to an end and I was facing the prospect of signing on. I didn't want to spend my life waiting for money from Pete. I wanted to be able to say that I could support Jess myself. I needed to be that role model for her. I needed to start believing in myself again. I might have been in a council flat, but I wanted to be paying them rent. There was no way I was going to get stuck in the housing benefit rut. That job opportunity was the trigger I needed to get me back out of the fog and into the real world again.

It was so good to be back working. For the first time in two years I allowed myself to feel proud of myself. Things with Pete were at a stalemate. One calm day, he called me and asked to see me. He sounded relaxed and said he wanted to meet me for lunch and go through everything. I wasn't that sure what he meant, but I assumed it was about when he would see Jess. He took me to the pub for lunch. We sat down and he started to talk. It was all the usual stuff. He was going to get help. He knew that he had issues with containing his 'frustrations' and would get help. He asked me if I would consider going to Relate together. I had heard it all before, and to be honest, I just didn't want to be sitting there. He started to creep me out. It's a very strange feeling to go from being desperate to please someone to then feeling a bit pukey when they look you in the eye. Very strange. I let him talk. I did a lot of nodding. I didn't want to disagree with him, not because I wanted to make him happy but because I wanted to get out of there without a scene. Which would have been ok – if he hadn't then got down on one knee.

Yes. There, in the same pub where we had met on that fateful Saturday night, Pete got down on one knee and asked me to marry him. The waitress and barman were watching and smiling. I grabbed his elbow and tried to pull him up, begging him not to do it. It was too late. The words had left his mouth and he was in front of me on one knee holding a princess-cut diamond. Oh God, no.

I can tell you that the best way to work out for definite if you really do want to be with someone or not is to have them propose. I felt sick to the stomach. No. No no no no. This was not my happy-ever-after. This was not my prince. This was not my Captain von Trapp.

I didn't trust him not to hurt me. He didn't make me feel safe. The love I felt from him was intermittent, and even at those times that I did believe he loved me, it was as if it was too much to handle. It was like forgetting to add salt to your food for days, and when you do remember, you have to eat all of the salt you forgot to add at once – all in one big bowl of soup. It was almost impossible to digest.

It was as though the diamond in that ring cut through the strings he had been using to play me. There and then, I told him that it was over. I knew that I was going to be just fine on my own. Jess and me in our little flat. We were going to be just fine.

Lessons in Life

Fish

Believe me, finding love was very much one of the furthest things from my mind. My daily routine involved getting up, getting Jessica to the childminder, and getting myself to work.

It would be nice to be able to tell you that I never heard from Pete again, but there are no prizes for guessing that the bonkers side of him hadn't quite run its course. Once he started to compute the reality that we were never going to be the peachy family unit he thought he desired, he thoroughly kicked the crazy up a gear.

Now, for those of you who have ever been in a similar situation, you will know that one of the hardest things to deal with is the fact that often the perpetrator genuinely has no understanding that what they are doing is wrong. It was standard practice for me to come home to the answerphone blinking. Anything over nine messages would mean that more than ten messages had been left. They would all be from Pete. Some angry, some frustrated, some sorry. It was hard being alone in the flat. He would often come knocking at my door at night. That I could largely deal with and ignore. What you can't ignore is someone spending hours systematically knocking on each window and shouting a combination of 'I love you' and 'You're a fucking slag' through the letter box.

He was often found on the corner of the street where I worked. He would follow me home, shouting his usual combination of expletives and declarations of love. I distinctly remember that my sister was staying with me once, which threw him completely as he was greeted by her picking up our daughter instead of me. She told him he had to stop all of this. Apparently, he looked her hard in the eye and responded: 'I love her'. To which my sister, baffled, shouted back at him: 'That doesn't make all of this ok!'

There it was. The issue. Somehow, someone can think that being in love is an excuse for anything. Stalking. Control. Abuse. It isn't. Perhaps the lesson in all of this was the power of love (*Back to the Future* reference unintended).

So, you are probably reading this and wondering why I still didn't get the police involved. It's a complicated reply that sounds a bit silly when I type it out. I just could never quite put us in the position of restricting his access to Jessica. Not for him, but for our daughter. Somewhere deep down, I just knew that he would never hurt her and by starting the proceedings for a restraining order I would be starting something that I wasn't sure I would have the strength to finish. Despite the fear, the loneliness and the confusion, I kept a clarity about how I had to deal with the situation. Not the situation around the relationship that Pete and I had, but the one that Jessica and Pete had. You only get one dad.

Saying that, life for me couldn't go on as it was. I was (for want of a better word) knackered. I was completely exhausted from it all. I tried to get away when I could, but as I was working full-time it wasn't always that easy.

One evening I had a call from my friend Anne. We had kept in touch since school and although we didn't see each other very often, we had remained good friends. On this particular occasion she invited me to come and stay with her at her dad's house for the weekend. Unusually for me at the time, I accepted without hesitation. That weekend I hopped on a train with Jess. Anne picked us up from the station. The moment I saw her my body flooded with pure relief.

Her dad's house was a stunning chocolate box cottage set in the middle of the most beautiful English countryside. Sadly, not quite remote enough to be unable to get a phone signal. During our stay, I continued to receive the usual barrage of texts from Pete. One thing was different. I was two hundred miles away with Jessica and felt safe. I was in the company of a true friend. Anne had known me since I was thirteen. She knew the real me. For the first time in what felt like forever, I let myself relax. Jess had a wonderful time too. Anne's dad treated her like a granddaughter and she adored toddling around the nearby paddocks. That weekend we felt like we were part of a secure family unit. I felt so safe that I even managed to find a sense of humour about it all. I would read out some of the texts periodically to Anne, noting the slightly more irrational ones and being entertained as any logical thread started to diminish. Well, that was until one particular one came through. Anne's face said it all. She just looked at me and said: 'I think it's time you got the police involved. That's not ok.'

The text referred to him finding me and raping me, 'just how I like it'.

It's odd how you can be so deep into your own normality of life that you get such a strange perception of what is acceptable or not. Anne was right. It was turning into written direct threats that I couldn't ignore. Without Anne's concern and understanding that weekend, who knows how long I would have remained blind to the reality of the situation I was in.

When I got back home, I didn't do anything initially. However, it was an important turning point. The next time he came knocking at all of my windows, I caved in.

Luckily for me, the neighbours verified his behaviour. As I started to go through what had been going on, piece by piece, I knew both by hearing my own voice out loud and by the reaction of the police that I had done the right thing. The right thing both for me and for Jessica. The police took statements and told me to put together transcripts of any texts I had received and any letters he had put through my door. I was still firmly convinced that I didn't want it to turn into a restraining order scenario. To this day, I am not sure how or why, but I had a gut feeling that this was probably about as far as it was going to go. Rightly or wrongly, I still felt that nothing that had happened was worth jeopardising Jessica's relationship with her father.

The police went straight from my flat to his. I had absolutely no idea what to expect from it. I had no idea what they were even going round there for. I didn't have to wait long to find out. An hour or so later, I got a call. They had found him at his house with no problem. In fact, he had invited them in and had happily verified everything that I had said. To be clear, not in a confessional 'it's a fair cop' style, but in a matter-of-fact way with no indication that he thought any of his behaviour was unacceptable. They recounted to me how they'd had to sit him down and explain to him that his behaviour towards me was unacceptable and could lead to serious consequences if he didn't leave me alone. To be honest, they seemed as baffled as I felt exhausted.

They reiterated my options and told me not to hesitate to call 999 if I felt in any serious danger. It was all a bit surreal. Things that I had thought were just something I had to deal with were now being seen as serious threats. For the past few years, I had been swimming around in my little tank, unwilling and unable to acknowledge that I had been living an unnecessarily fearful existence. Now my eyes had been opened. There was a serious crack in my little goldfish bowl and I had to jump back out of it and into the big sea of the real world. The thing is, I wasn't scared. I felt safer than I had done in three years.

Thankfully, things calmed down a bit after that. I changed my mobile number, so at least the texts and mobile calls were stopped. Sometimes he would seem to disappear off the face of the planet; at other times he would start excessively calling the landline again. He seemed to genuinely care about Jessica, but it was very hard for me to let him see her. I always worried that one day I would let him take her out for the afternoon and that it would be the last time I saw her. I know that sounds dramatic, but that's how I felt. I am certain that it was me he had the problem with and no one else, but I couldn't be certain that he wouldn't use her as a weapon. I needed time and proof through his actions that I could trust him. It wasn't quite the end of all the issues, but now I had let the outside world in to cast their eyes over the curdled mess that was the relationship between Pete and me, I could start to consider the possibility of starting again.

So, how do you get on with life and love after a situation like the one I had with Pete? I can't give you a straight answer to that. The best way I can describe how I felt is completely and utterly lost.

I suddenly found myself back at the beginning. It was like a *Men in Black*-style mind blank had been performed on me in respect of everything I had learnt about love and self-worth. It was like I had absolutely no idea what I wanted, what I was supposed to want, and what was expected of me. I don't think it ever occurred to me whether it mattered how I felt at all.

The months passed by. Despite Pete being 'on the scene' in a bonkers way only a few months ago, we had actually been split up for around a year. I know I might sound a bit tragic, but honestly, I kept in pretty good spirits over those months. I was only twenty-five. It is a huge cliché, but I genuinely concentrated on my daughter and making her feel safe and happy. I had (and still do have) the most fabulous friends, all of whom appreciated TV karaoke as much as I did. Ok, so I might have been completely off the market in the love stakes, but I most definitely wasn't ready to shove my head in the oven just yet.

I was now working for a local firm. I missed running the tutoring centre and I missed teaching, but the business was being sold and I had to move on. The timing was pretty good. I was able to move on to a more secure working environment. I didn't have to worry about Pete turning up at the office, where I had often been working alone. I was now working in an environment full of people – men people, women people. I was just so happy to be surrounded by a support network again.

As for the job? The work was dull as shit. I was supposed to be an administrator, but the reality was that the only administrative tasks I was given were opening the post and picking up the phone. I did everything I could to keep the work hours ticking by. I can confirm that photocopying your boobs is quite difficult to do discreetly. FYI, for the best results, cover yourself with a coat as your boobs are pressed on the photocopy panel. I definitely had more success photocopying my face. Ok, so you risk severely damaging your eyesight, but the results are bloody funny. You'll also find out just how much you can look like Sloth from The Goonies.

After the years and months of vulnerability, it was so nice to be able to start new relationships again without any of the pressures. It was so nice to have all the sexual connotations taken away and meet men just as friends again.

The last time I'd felt like that was when I started university. Men were friends, not potential boyfriends. Although I had still maintained strong female friendships, being with Pete had made it too hard to maintain male friendships. I was so lucky to find that job at that time.

I had the most random and friendly colleagues. Within the first few days of working there, Harry had regaled me with the story of when he realised Terry Wogan had stolen one of his jokes. I mean – come on. What's not to love about that? Then there was Adam. He was a diamond. He was like an older brother. He made me laugh such a lot and properly looked after me. It was Adam who stepped up the day Pete had a dozen roses delivered to my desk. He smashed them to pieces in the car park in an appreciated, symbolic gesture of comradeship. It was a tough situation for me to be in. No one wants to have to tell their line manager about a slightly unbalanced ex-partner who may or may not pop in from time to time for a bit of intimidation. Still, I had to. I will always be grateful to them. I received nothing but support from everyone.

The bonds and friendships that I formed at that time were more important to me than I understood at the time – particularly those that I formed with my male colleagues. I now understand that they were intrinsic in helping me start to see that perhaps I wasn't the crazy one after all. Maybe it was

Pete making me believe what he wanted me to believe. After all, if I could make friends with boys, then who knows – maybe one day I could just about make a decent girlfriend.

Despite the flickering of positive thought, I was a very long way from even considering trying to peek at another willy. It was nice to believe that somewhere very deep down inside me there might be some scraps of girlfriend material. I was genuinely content in my little world. A happy daughter, a positive working environment and my sweet little flat. Although I had technically been single for a year or so, I was still a long way off considering another relationship. For a start, I was a mum now. Do people go on dates with people who have children? If you have children, do you tell your date? If you don't tell them, are you lying? If you do tell them, are they most likely going to turn out to be a massive paedo? If I did meet someone and Pete found out, would he hunt them down, stab them in the face and make bird feed balls out of their testicles?

There was a lot to think about. Mainly 948,563 reasons not to even consider trying to meet anyone else. The thing is, though, I was lonely. All was fine and full of candyfloss in the daytime, but the moment Jessica went to bed, I was alone. As completely pathetic as it sounds, there was a testosterone-scented hole in my life that I didn't quite know how to fill (pun probably intended).

So, how do you go from toying with the notion of putting yourself out there to filling in an online dating application? Well, for a start, just choosing what sort of website to go for is a minefield. For those of you who are new to all this, I will give you a little overview of the range of dating websites that are out there. They tend to be categorised as follows:

Free sites:
Why not? A good place to start. They involve very little investment in both time and money and have the widest range of singles. A word of warning about free sites, though. They also have the most nutters. If you can overlook the people asking if they can cum in your hair and are prepared for spelling such as 'gawjus', go with it. Remember, you are normal, so chances are there are other relatively normal singles on the site also looking for love.

Targeted sites:
I succumbed to this once and signed up to muddymatches.com. A site for 'country folk'. I admit it does sound a bit like a site for meeting someone who likes pooing on glass tables. I had a romantic image of transforming myself into a buxom farmer's wife – maybe Ma Larkin, but hopefully less fat. I chatted for a while to a potato

farmer. He was ok until I sent him a picture of a tub of Smash that I found in my parents' food cupboard. I never heard from him again. I did meet one chap. Think *Made in Chelsea* meets Old MacDonald. Now, I can cope with a certain level of posh, but when he said he was heading home after our lunch date to 'cook a partridge for his fellows', I had to bail.

Paid sites:
Sadly, the days of free sites are slipping away and the vast majority need you to hand cash over. They all lie and say it's free. You join and then get told you need to pay in order to see messages/profiles/your own reflection. Having to pay does have the bonus of filtering out some of the video masturbators (some, not all ... they lurk amongst us like a dirty *X-Files*). It can also be a bit depressing when you've paid £15 and the most appealing person is someone balancing lager in an empty trainer. (I'll come back to him later.)

Long-winded sites:
You know the ones. They advertise on TV. For a start, the fact that they advertise on TV shows they charge shitloads. They have impossibly attractive couples waxing lyrical about the magic of the site. They are normally walking on the

beach/in the woods, often with a dog. Sort of like Poligrip adverts for young people. I never had the patience to do the application. These sites send you recommended 'matches'. Um. No thanks. Spending four hours filling in what flavour of Opal Fruit describes me best and explaining why Ginger Spice was my favourite Spice Girl, only to be sent profiles of people who would be fitting for NHS gonorrhoea information leaflets was not for me. Saying that, for those who are far less shallow than I am, they are apparently brilliant.

Specialised sites:
These are exceedingly specific – I'm talking sites for people looking for a precise type of partner. For example, people who only want old lady sex or fatties. I came across one site myself: sugardaddies.com. Ooh – maybe I could find love *and* sort out a few money worries? The site seemed to take applications from young women with nice boobs who were looking for an older man. In my innocence, it conjured up images of Maria and Captain von Trapp. The trouble was, I was no nun. With excited anticipation, I sent my application off. They never responded. Rude. As it happens, I have learnt since that it was less about lonely older men looking for their nuns, and a little more about sweaty rich chaps looking for young women to spank for cash. Fair enough if that's your

cup of tea, but I preferred to hang on for something a little more like a fairy tale.

So what did I go for first? Well, one long Saturday night, an advert for a website came on the TV. I can't remember which one it was for. I do remember wondering why anyone would pay £20 a month to meet up with a sex offender. Curiosity got the better of me, and before I knew it I was dialling up the internet and typing 'free dating sites' into the search engine. I mean, if I was probably only going to meet sex offenders, I wasn't going to pay for it.

www.plentyoffish.com

Nowadays it is called 'POF' and is as well-known as Tinder, but in those days it was a whole new weird and wonderful world. On the plus side, it was completely free to use. No doubt they were selling all my details on, but hey ho – I was fine with that. That night, I didn't sign up, but I had a good look through what there was out there for me. I was quietly impressed. At least half of the ones I clicked on seemed ok. I mean, truth be known, I've have never had a 'type'. Also, I was happy to look at ages ranging from twenty to fifty, which didn't half open things up. Let's face it – I had just come out of a relationship with someone who was genuinely old enough to be my dad. Who was I to be fussy? The next evening, I pulled the metaphorical plaster off and started to put together a profile. First problem? A photo. No smartphones then. If you were lucky, you had a couple of scanned pics of you in a nice frock from a wedding or two. Even better, you had access to a digital camera. I had a digital camera. It was shit and the battery lasted around forty-five minutes, but it had a timer and was compatible with my crap old laptop. It's funny to see the young 'uns now. I know how old people feel when they see people my age thinking we invented kinky sex. Teenagers believe they invented 'selfies'. In fact, those of us who have dabbled in the internet dating world have been doing 'selfies' for years. The only difference is that we called it 'taking a photo of yourself'. Plus, we did it not so much for flattery and universal praise and attention but for practical reasons. You need a decent set of pics to reel in the messages. No one (including me) is interested in a profile without a picture. For me, it's not so much because I am hugely superficial (I'm not. Well, maybe a bit.) but more importantly to make sure I don't already know the person who is messaging me. Trust me, it's not a great feeling to read a mildly offensive private message from someone asking to put their finger up your bottom and then realise that it's from your elderly postman.

I know this doesn't go along with the 'we're all in the same boat' comradeship attitude to dating, but I genuinely didn't want to meet anyone. I needed a few months of romantic Dutch courage. If I was being truthful, I wanted to hear that there were men out there who thought I was pretty – or at least pretty enough to want to see without the lights low on a dimmer switch. I designed very straightforward criteria for myself. I limited who I would converse with to men who were stationed abroad with the Forces. The majority of these turned out to be homesick soldiers stuck out on tour in Afghanistan. I thought of myself as a modern-day Vera Lynn, but with less singing and more suggestive references to seeing my nipples.

I know what you're thinking – you and your dirty mind. You have visions of me typing away to lots of chaps on different screens like some instant messenger gang-bang. Well, that wasn't what it was like. If I liked the initial message from someone, then we would get chatting on instant messenger. Ok, so I wasn't particularly loyal – but I would be for the times that I was messaging that one person. Um, and yes – I would be lying if I said that none of the discussions revolved around them banging me against a wall, but actually a lot of them wanted to talk about home. The ones who wanted to chat before asking for nipples always stood out in my mind. Particularly the ones who wanted to know what I had been up to, what supermarket beer offers were on, and who Ian might marry next in *EastEnders*. I always got the impression that these were probably the genuinely single ones. You have to remember that some of these guys are out there for weeks and months at a time. It's all very well if they have a wife or girlfriend to speak to back home, but being single and out on tour must be so much more shit.

For all the straight women who are a bit unsure about getting back out there and onto the dating scene again, I highly recommend the approach I used. You get the attention and the butterflies, but you feel completely safe. They are far away with nothing better to do than talk to women who they find attractive and who may or may not be willing to send them a picture of their boobs. It's very much a two-way, win/win situation. I never gave out personal information, so I didn't worry about having to reveal my status as a 'single parent'. I was just me. I hadn't felt like 'just me' in a long time.

 I can't say that a couple didn't raise my curiosity a little more than others. One chap I talked to fairly regularly was like a cartoon fantasy. Ryan was six feet four inches tall, tanned, dark, and ridiculously muscly. Not muscly in that painful-looking, six-pack way, but muscly in the same vein as Arnie in *Twins*. As you already know, that's my dream

Arnie (*sigh*). What on Earth he would have seen in me, I have no idea, although at that age I was probably at my peak. I was tall, blonde, tanned and a size 12. Unless I ingested a tapeworm, that was about as slim as I was ever going to get. Our chats even got as far as him confiding in me that he was single and had a daughter back in the UK. I didn't tell him about Jessica. I didn't need to. It was a great moment for me, though. I realised at that moment that I wasn't the only one. For the past few months, I had felt alone on the little island of Single Parent. Just hearing one other date-worthy person telling me that they were single with a child was a huge turning point. Just maybe it would be ok for me to consider being a girlfriend again. Not right now, perhaps – but soon.

    I confided in a few friends about my toe-dipping into the world of dating. My friend Hannah was also single and not really looking for anything serious. I told her about how I kept commitment at a distance by only chatting to chaps who I was never going to have to see. I explained how it satisfied a mutual need for company and attention. Hannah signed up and soon we were comparing notes on our recent chat buddies and sending each other pics of ourselves for approval prior to posting. It was so fab and such a relief to be able to talk about it to someone who understood the weird world that I was now in. Believe me, at that time, internet dating was not the commonplace activity it is now. It wasn't quite grubby confused singles ads at the back of the Evening Telegraph, but it wasn't seen as much better.

One evening, Hannah and I were sitting together going through our new messages. A new message popped up in her inbox with a picture of a shiny, tanned, topless man and the message 'Am I man enough for you?'. It was Ryan.

Out of all of the thousands and thousands of people for him to message, he had picked the only other person I knew on there. It was either a massive coincidence or he was messaging a LOT of people at the same time. It felt like that horrible moment when you and a friend realise you have both snogged the same person in the past. You know it shouldn't matter, but it sort of does. It was at that point that I gave what I was doing a huge rain check. It felt like a little blinking red light. I was immediately reminded that as safe as I might feel about it, it was all bollocks.

I put plentyoffish on the back burner for a while. I had been on there for a good few weeks, but if I had kept it going much longer, I might have started to believe that the chats I was having with people on there could lead to something more. All of a sudden, I could sort of see how seemingly normal women end up in love and engaged to someone on death row. Loneliness has a lot to answer for.

Safe

I decided to put the world of virtual dating on hold for a bit. I didn't get out much. I had no babysitting opportunities and no urge to face the real world, so it suited me fine. One grey afternoon, the chaps in accounting were flirting with the idea of speed dating and asked if I would join them. I genuinely couldn't think of anything worse. The idea of having to be continually (and repeatedly) interesting for three minutes and then be judged sounded awful. I could just about cope with being rejected in the virtual world of faux dating that I had created. I mean, you could argue that they didn't know the 'real you' and all that. Speed dating was a whole different ball game. I would have to face rejection by real people head-on. No thanks.

As luck would have it, a golden opportunity to go '*out*-out' was on the horizon. It was nearly Christmas. For the first time in my life, this also meant the office Christmas party. I decided to make the effort. I bagged myself some full-on childcare for the night. It was time for me to shine my shoes, dust off my stockings, and shove some mistletoe down my bra.

I pulled out all the stops. I mean, if I had a night to myself, then I was going to go for it. If there were chandeliers, I was going to be dangling off them. It started off as the standard Christmas party affair – a fancy meal in a private club. The meal passed by with no dramatic incidents. I was starting to get the vino well and truly down my neck. It was 'situation normale'. I kept myself in check. Well, I thought I did. After the meal, we were having drinks at the bar when a colleague (you know 'that' colleague, aka party-pooper) advised me to slow down with my drinking. Did I? Did I bollocks. I told her to sod off, sat down at the adjacent table, and drank a stranger's pint. It was beginning to turn into 'that' sort of evening. Remember, I might have been a mum now, but underneath it all, I was like any other twenty-five-year-old single woman needing a break from being relatively sensible.

Romance – or even just a bit of nakedness – was the furthest thing from my mind. Or so I thought. Until Tom. We had always got on fairly well at work. He was one of a couple of single guys in the office. He was divorced and a little quiet but had a good sense of humour and was good-looking. Until around midnight on the night of the office party, I had no idea that I fancied him. Maybe the booze awoke the suppressed lustful feelings I had for him deep down in my loins. Or maybe I was just pissed. Who knows? I do know that I wanted to do something about it. I saw him on the dance floor and something just snapped. Knowing that this opportunity wasn't going to come again, in the deep blue lights of the sticky-floored club, I locked, loaded and launched on him. Classy.

All of my anxiety, fear, frustration, and vulnerability melted away in that one moment. He was a fantastic kisser and I was pissed as a fart.

He was a modern-day gentleman, to some extent. Right from the start, he was keen to make sure that I hadn't made a huge mistake. He kept repeating that he thought I had only decided to kiss him because he was single and had children, too, and thus seemed like the 'safe' option. That wasn't in my thoughts at the time. I just fancied him and was a bit pissed. Pure and simple.

I know what you're thinking. Something along the lines of 'don't dip your pen in the office ink' perhaps? I agree. It is a saying for a bloody good reason. If you want to get it together with someone at work, you'd better be bloody sure it's heading for party rings and nappies or you'll end up spending the next few years hiding in the stationery cupboard until they've left the photocopy room. Needless to say, I hadn't quite given it that much thought.

What followed on from that night was one long hangover. It wasn't just about getting the booze out of my system. No. I was about to start a forty-eight-hour wait to go to work on the Monday morning. A two-day wait to face Tom again. He never asked for my number and I never gave him it. This was my first bad sign.

Luckily (or not), we worked in different areas of the office, so I didn't have to face him straightaway. The minutes ticked by. Ninety minutes, to be precise. Nothing. Not an email, not a chance walk past my desk. Nothing. Maybe he wasn't such a gentleman. I felt like a complete penis. Still, in for a penny, in for a pound. I decided to pop him an email:

`'Any regrets?'`

'Ping'. He replied within seconds.

`'None at all.'`

Phew.

And that, as they say, was the beginning. Unbeknown to me, that Friday night was to be the start of something a little longer term. It wasn't the plan. I had no plans. He seemed to like me and I liked him. Due to us both having our own family commitments, we saw each other fairly infrequently. As we worked together, though, we made what we could of it. He was keen to keep things quiet in the office. I was fine with that. It made it more interesting. As you know, I was normally bloody bored at work. To be honest, after the complexity of things with Pete it was nice just to enjoy mutual affection. It was uncomplicated. It was nice.

Little did I realise at the time, but I was a bit nuts. Everything that had happened with Pete was still fairly fresh. That – mixed with my general mid-twenties vibrancy, stamina and lack of adult experience – made me a challenging combination. Challenging is putting it mildly. Perhaps it's a general lesson for all of you chaps out there in their thirties and forties who might fantasise about bagging themselves the young, blonde receptionist. Maybe even one who has been told off for wearing skirts to work which are too short. (This did actually happen to me. To date, it is the strangest work meeting I have ever had.) I was a bit bonkers. No, not in that cutesy Zooey Deschanel/sober Drew Barrymore way. I was exceedingly hard work. Needy. Very needy. Honestly, chaps – be careful what you wish for.

On top of my neediness, he also had to deal with Pete, who was still in the background and still being bonkers. I was still getting the excessive landline messages that flitted from being angry to sorry to regretful and then back to angry. Despite that, Tom was very understanding. After a few months, I let him meet Jessica. He was great with her and she liked him. It meant we could see more of each other. But more than that it, it was nice to feel part of a 'real' family unit. Anyone who has been a single parent will understand what I mean by that.

I might have had my issues and barriers, but he seemed like he was happy with me. I would love to say that we were lost souls, now joined together by our love of chess and exotic cheese. The reality is that he was probably so keen on me because of all the sex. It had been a while. Not that he didn't know what he was doing. Far from it. When we started to sleep together with alarming regularity at the beginning, we hit an unusual problem. We had to take a break because he had friction burns on his knob. Honestly – friction burns. I had never seen this before and have never seen it since. Maybe he just needed it breaking in a bit? Who knows. Luckily, after that initial Sudocrem-requiring hurdle, things calmed down. Well, maybe not down. Things calmed 'up'. He was always there, ready for duty at any time the opportunity came up (pun intended). I can definitely say that when it came to sex, still waters ran deep. He was cracking in bed. No complaints there. Although he did make some very strange statements. I can never forget when he told me that he had visited prostitutes and that 'it was ok because they wash you and themselves before and after'. I remember trying not to look fazed. I hated the idea of looking the prude. He quickly broke into a smile and a laugh and said he was only joking. I'm still genuinely not sure.

That aside, I was feeling comfortable. Safe and comfortable. It was such a relief to be with someone who I felt I could second-guess. It's an odd thing to be grateful for, but when you have had to spend your days fearfully treading on eggshells, it's such a relief to be with someone and be confident that their mood will stay fairly stable. If I had a friend over, he would be polite. More importantly, when they left I didn't worry that he was going to suddenly explode about something he had seen or heard and suppressed all evening. It was such a relief.

Although being with Tom was a big relief, it started to feel maybe a little too comfortable. As you know, when we first got together he questioned my motives and accused me of choosing him as the safe option. That was honestly not the case. For a start, that would have taken far too much thought, and at the time I had drunk enough Shiraz to float the Titanic. However, as time went on, it became more and more apparent that he might have been right.

In some ways, he was clearly the safe option. He was most definitely safe when it came to money. For want of a gentler description, he was as tight as a duck's arse. This wasn't such a bad thing. The last thing I needed was to be with someone who craved the champagne lifestyle while I was on a SodaStream paycheck. I didn't want his money. Crikey, no. Far from it. My need to be an independent single mother was carved into my very being. I would have hated the idea of needing someone else to rely on to help me look after Jess and manage on a daily basis. I was quite capable of doing that myself, thank you very much. No, it wasn't about day-to-day money, it was the unfulfilled suggestions and promises. He was forever talking about things we would do. We would go away for the weekend to the country house near where he lived. We would go back to that Thai restaurant we went to once when we first got together. I could drip on. Did we ever do any of those things? Did we bollocks. It was all talk. If I got a pound for every time he mentioned us going to New York, we could have both gone. Twice. First Class. He did buy me a New York guidebook once. That's not really the same. I guess broken promises were free.

At that time, I had no idea what I should expect from a partner and love. I knew I didn't want to be frightened. I knew I didn't want to feel insecure. I didn't feel either of those things. I thought that was all I needed and all I deserved. Still, as undemanding as I was, there were a few things that made the little alarm bells ring at the back of my mind. I look back on them now and they set off honking great fire alarm blares. Ok, so the strangest thing was that in the entire time we were together, he never fitted a door on his bathroom. I was pretty convinced it wasn't because he was a sex offender. It was more that he just never got around to doing anything. Talking about when and where we were going to visit restaurants and holiday destinations was one thing. Not getting around to putting a door back on the bathroom is another. He was in the middle of home improvement work and had taken it off its hinges. I never complained. At the time, I was so desperate not to be without him at my own flat that I was happy to put up with a doorless toilet at his place. I certainly wasn't prepared to start laying down demands. Now I look back on it and realise that it is perfectly reasonable to ask for someone to fit the door back on their bathroom so that you don't have to lean down to avoid the neighbours opposite seeing you on the toilet.

The sad reality of our relationship was that it wasn't good at all. It wasn't just the empty promises and my colossal neediness. He had a bit of a shitty streak. I was never sure if I was being paranoid, but I felt like he would occasionally do very strange things in order to keep some sort of control. I always felt that he used my experience with Pete against me. Of course, it could be that I distorted it all in my head and it wasn't the case, but there was one definite incident. He had a rolled-up newspaper in his hand and raised it towards me during a row. I flinched. He went bananas about how he wasn't like Pete and screamed at me for putting me in the same bracket. It was the screaming reaction that bothered me, not the newspaper.

I don't want to paint him as a bad guy. He really wasn't. He was fine. I was lost and confused. He was dull. I might have been fine with that at the time we got together, but deep down inside, there was the old me – gagged and bound but desperate to make a reappearance when she felt ready. After nearly two years with Tom, she was ready to come out again.

To say he was dull is a bit harsh. Beige. He was very beige. He was beige and I was beginning to feel repressed. In May, I had my annual 'Come dressed representing your favourite European country and dig into the rude food buffet' Eurovision party. The next day, a good friend of mine pretty much summed up our problems with one question:

'Who was the random guy in the corner dressed as Father Christmas who didn't speak to anyone?'

'Um. That's Tom. We've been together for eighteen months!'

That evening, Tom and I both learnt lessons. He learnt that if there was a fancy dress party, he should pull his finger out of his bottom and find his own costume or he would end up dressed as Father Christmas in May. I learnt that I needed more than him. We'd had some good times, but I knew it could never last. I needed a sprinkle of glitter and someone who understood my needs. When I say needs, I'm not talking marriage and diamond rings. I mean someone who would happily slow-dance to The Muppets in the living room and maybe someone who was willing to take more risks – like investing more than £5 on a toilet seat.

We broke up.

The truth is that he was completely right from the start. I think subconsciously I did go for him that night because he seemed safe. The thing is, I am a live wire. I was as a child, I was in my teens, I was before Pete, and I continue to be so now. He wasn't.

Maybe I should never even have considered a relationship at that time. Certainly, one that was the crapped-out remnants of a drunken office party. Maybe our relationship was just poo rolled in glitter after all. After everything that had happened with Pete, I lost who I was for a while. To add to the complexities, I was also suddenly a single parent. I had no idea what I should expect or want from a relationship and even whether I should be able to have romantic relationships anymore. You know that your children are the centre of your world and that your own needs have to go on the back burner. It takes a while to realise that – single parent or not – everyone has the right to find love.

I sound like I regret my time with Tom, but that's not true. I know, looking back, that had I not have not had my time with Pete, I wouldn't have been interested in Tom. I certainly would not have stayed with him as long as I did. We had some nice times together. His parents were so kind to me and, as irrelevant as that might sound, that made such a difference. I felt part of a full family unit. It was nice. The fact that things between Tom and I weren't perfect actually made it the perfect thing for me at that time. I had to admit to myself that I wasn't ready. Being with Tom helped me get back on my way to discover who I was again, and I will always be grateful for that.

After Tom, I was fine. We had already started to bicker more and more. That safe little bubble I thought I was in was about to burst. He knew we were heading for shitsville, too. Sometimes you both know it has to end and it's just a matter of who gets in there first. In this case, it was me.

I definitely wasn't interested in another relationship. One thing my time with Tom taught me was that I was not ready. Far from it. I felt like I needed to start again. I needed a proper break from men. I needed to do a bit of retraining.

Blind

Unbeknown to me, five years of dating now lay ahead of me. Some liaisons would last minutes, some weeks, some a few months. I kept Jessica out of it. She met two of my dates over those five years. They were the ones I genuinely felt were a long-term prospect. Aside from the safety aspect, I didn't ever want to hear the question: 'Mummy – whatever happened to Uncle Bob/Ian/James/Kevin/Moses?'

Now, four years after our final break-up, Pete had changed. He wasn't perfect, but he seemed to have a handle on his emotions. He also had a new, clearer relationship with someone else and even another child on the way. It took time to rebuild trust, but I genuinely liked his new partner and he seemed different. Calmer. Collected. I am not sure how or why. Maybe time was the healer. Maybe it was the perspective of a new partner which made him happier that changed things. Whatever it was, I started to relent and allow him time with Jessica. Eventually, we developed a routine. Jess would spend an evening a week with him and his new family. Little by little, I started to get a bit of 'me' time again. In addition to that one night a week, occasionally Jess would go to stay for a week or so with my parents over the holidays or for a few days with my sister and her family. It gave me a break and a chance to be me, the single lady and not me, the single mum, for a bit.

I knew that in the long term I wasn't going to be fulfilled by inane MSN chats with soldiers. I had to graduate to 'real life'. There was only so much updating strangers on *EastEnders* I could deal with, and it certainly wasn't going to get me any snogs.

It is not like I agreed to go on every date knowing that it was not going to work out. I genuinely put myself out there in order to find the True Love that seemed to have eluded me so far. I still had faith. It might have been hiding really quite deep down in my soul, but faith that I would find True Love was definitely still there.

They say that every journey starts with a single step. Well, my dating journey started with a single date. Full of genuine positivity and enthusiasm, I forged ahead into the unknown, always hoping that the next man I met would make sense of my feelings and my needs. The next man would be the one. The fairy tale romance.

Of course, if the first chap I met had been that person, this would be the end of my little book – so there are no prizes for guessing that it took a little bit longer than I had hoped. It's a good job, really. I probably didn't know it at the time, but I needed those dates. The disasters, the comedy moments, the questionable smells. I needed them all to relearn everything that I thought I already knew. Each one taught me a little bit more about myself and a little bit more about how I could be a better person. Well, maybe not the now (relatively) well-known public figure who turned up to our date with a knuckleduster. I'll leave him out of this.

 I figured that for my first 'go' I should push the boat out and join match.com. I reasoned that having to pay to sign up would filter out at least a few of the kamikaze masturbators. The pool wasn't overflowing with fish, but there were one or two who seemed perky enough. Dance-Off was immediately appealing. He regaled me with tales of dance-offs with friends. Ooh, and he was a fireman. Well, there was a picture of him in a fireman's outfit – and he gave me his word he wasn't just a stripper with an eye for detail.

 If anyone was ever under the impression that I blame others for my own shortcomings, my first internet dating meet-up situation most certainly proves otherwise. Yes, this first date was dripping full of 'don't' lessons. I could probably write an entirely separate book on everything I shouldn't have done that night. I've just picked out the significant highlights, or, as I see them, buttock-clenching lowlights.

I made an effort. No, I mean I thoroughly made an effort. I have no idea who I thought I was. A low-rent Jodie Marsh springs to mind. New, black Chinese silk dress, new underwear, gel nails. I mean, gel nails? He was based a couple of hours' drive away, so I suggested a hotel he could stay in. It had a stunning 1920s-style cocktail lounge bar and I was a sucker for a vodka Martini at the time. Yes, I know. Meeting a stranger for 40% proof drinks dressed as a reasonably priced prostitute was my first mistake.

I chatted with the taxi driver on my way to meet him. I told him I was going on a date with a chap I had met through a dating website. We pulled up to the hotel and (I kid you not) as I handed him his fare he looked at me with a serious expression and said:

'Be careful. Loads of people get raped or murdered by people they've met through internet dating. I'm sure you'll be fine, though ...'

With those heady words of comfort, I went in to meet my date. As I walked in, I had a sudden panic. Not because I thought he wouldn't turn up, but because I had actually never spoken to him. It had all been via text and email. I vowed then to always have an actual phone call prior to any date. I thought I was about to meet someone who might talk like Jamie Oliver after a night out.

I recognised him immediately. He was smartly dressed in a shirt and suit trousers. He smelt gorgeous and there was no trace of a comedy voice. I was relieved. He seemed relieved. We ordered cocktails and sat and chatted.

It felt easy, although my standard of behaviour started to dwindle fairly early on. He had a bit of a 'wide boy' feel to him, which I started to find hilarious. When I was in the toilets on my 'I've not been stabbed yet' phone check to my friend, I began doing borderline offensive impressions of him. When I got back to him at our table I continued, waving my arms and saying: 'yoooooor in *EastEnderrrrrrs*'. Before long, I was asking him to repeat phrases such as 'I'm Danny Dyer, and I'm a litl' bit nawteee'. Which he did.

I suggested we explored some bars nearby. I say 'bars'. A strip club. I was so worried about seeming dull that I went at it like Father Christmas on coke at a beard convention. As it happens, Dance-Off wasn't that up for a night in Spearmint Thigh-No. Another lesson learnt – the person who suggests a strip club for a drink on a first date is rarely marriage material. I then had a worse idea. I suggested we popped back to see my flat.

This is when it started to get silly.

Almost as soon as we walked through my front door, I realised it wasn't what I wanted. I turned to him and demanded we went back out into town. We called the taxi back and went all the way back.

We went back to the hotel. Inspired by my Chinese dress and the thirty-four vodka Martinis, I thought it would be a brilliant idea to pretend to be in a James Bond film. Depressingly, this seemed to just involve me hiding from Dance-Off and pointing gun fingers at him.

When I found myself stripping down to my extravagant underwear and chasing a bellboy down a corridor, I finally realised it was no longer a date. I was subconsciously in a *Carry On* film.

It was around this time that he said he'd take me home. I was relieved. I was exhausted from all the effort. And vodka. I'll miss out telling you about any cheeky kisses with Dance-Off. I'd still like you to only think of him as the gentleman to my tragic state.

We chatted the next day. He was a good guy and in many respects the perfect person for my first internet date. Still, it was never going to work between us. Partly because he lived too far away, but mainly because I'd acted like I was on day release when we met.

He gave me some solid man advice:
'If you think all men are going to treat you like shit, then they will treat you like shit.'

He had a bloody good point. He knew exactly what my game was. The date was one huge assumption that I wasn't going to get anywhere just as me. I knew there and then that in the future I had to present myself as I was. Ok – maybe a filtered version for the first date. Deep down there is definitely a Benny Hill's Angel I have to keep hidden. I am not all that sure I am alone in that. I think we are all either busting to strip down to suspenders and chase a milkman, or really want to be chased. There's nothing wrong with that – I just needed to wait until at least the third date before *The Benny Hill Show* theme tune sounded.

So, needless to say, I realised not long after the date with Dance-Off that I had a lot of relearning to do. I hoped it was going to just involve a bit of a break and more careful consideration of who I chose to meet. As we are a fair way from the end of the book, you will have realised that it wasn't going to be that straightforward.

Considering everything that happened with Pete, you might have thought that I would run a mile from another 'older man' situation. Well, you know me. My thought-process didn't quite work like that. If they were nice, interested in me and could achieve a level of financial security marginally higher than an Elvis impersonator on Brighton Pier, I wasn't going to rule them out.

Let's call him Bodywarmer (an imaginative name, I know – I've chosen it because of the bodywarmer he wore in his profile picture). We met through plentyoffish.com (no expense spared). He seemed nice enough. Let's face it, my expectations and demands weren't always particularly high. This was one of those times. He was forty, and he had a job and his own teeth. He looked a bit like William Hague. That's not relevant to the story, although it does underline that this was a low point on the graph of my expectations.

After a fair bit of chatting for a couple of weeks, we decided to meet up for a drink. I chose a pub local to me, partly because I'd had a few non-starters lately and I couldn't be arsed to make much of an effort, and partly because I knew the barmaid and I thought she might notice if he tried to drug me and chop me up into little pieces in the car park.

He was pleasant enough, although part of me felt as though I had just met up with someone my dad worked with. He was older and very charming. We chatted. Well, we talked about him. The only point at which I became the topic of conversation was when it was about sex. This was ok with me at the time. I took it as a compliment. It also took place not long after a date with a chap who had tried to part my legs under the table, so just talking about sex seemed quite Victorian. (Of course, the leg-parter is a story and lesson in itself that I'll tell you about later.)

I felt comfortable with Bodywarmer, and he charmed me into a second date. This time, I got on the Shiraz train, and we did end up relatively naked. Ok. Very naked. Now this is something I will never forget, as when I say the only hair on his body was his armpits and eyebrows, I am not exaggerating. To quote Blackadder, his genitals looked like 'the last chicken in the shop'. Now, gentlemen. Unless you are a swimmer or a participant in similar sports, I don't recommend shaving off all of your pubic hair without prior suggestion. The only thing worse than this is men who shave the top of their pubes to try and make their willies look bigger. It doesn't work. It does, however, itch as it grows back. Everyone thinking you've contracted pubic lice is not a good look.

I digress.

By the time our third date came around, I started to realise he knew absolutely nothing about me. He'd talked about himself, so it never hit me that his intention could be anything other than to see how it went between us. I'd played the perfect host and made the required effort. When I got home after the date, I checked my phone. I flicked through my texts and realised that we were on two different pages of two different books. Mine was a lesser-known Mills & Boon, and his was Readers' Wives. So I texted him:

```
'Um - are you just using me for sex
until someone that is more appropriate
girlfriend material turns up?'
```
He responded later:
```
'Yes.'
```
Now, although in my heart I knew that he wasn't Ant to my Dec, this made me feel awful. I felt duped by his charm. It was representative of all those insecurities I had lurking. I thought at this point that no bloke ever wanted to know me as a person. He was unashamedly completely unapologetic. Now, I have had been involved in liaisons where we both knew it was a temporary thing. All cards on the table and both in agreement – and I have truly enjoyed it. This was different. I felt like a total tit. A very grubby loser.

So please. If your heart's not in it, that's fine, but I urge you to put your cards on the table. You know, it doesn't hurt to fake a little interest in the other person just to let them down gently. If you're willing to put your penis in them or have their penis in you, you should be willing to pay the compliment tax or the let-them-down-gently levy.

Love karma comes around. No less than eighteen months later, out of the blue, I had a text from Bodywarmer. As if nothing had happened. The usual sexual nonsense. I didn't respond. The next day, he texted an apology. He said he was drunk (flattering). I had the greatest pleasure to be able to respond – completely truthfully – as follows:

`'Ah, that's ok. My boyfriend and I found it hilarious.` I would've replied earlier but we were driving back from a weekend in Paris :-)'

It was a small victory for my former dating self, but it meant that I closed that particular dating episode as the winner. Ha. It's a little reminder to be kind to your dates. Treat them as you wish to be treated or love karma might bite you on the bottom.

On the subject of love karma, the little text conversation I had with Bodywarmer was nothing compared to what happened to Mr Pants.

Mr Pants comes under the category 'set-ups'. Any of you who have been single for longer than a few months will have definitely had friends and acquaintances offering suggestions of single people they know who you might hit it off with. I was not immune to this. Ok, some people hate the idea of being set up, but I quite liked it. If a friend knew us both, then chances are they wouldn't want to hook me up with a window-licking rapist.

The trouble is, nine times out of ten, the person setting you up has never dated said person. You might know the sweetest and most charming person – perfect to go on a date with someone you know. Perhaps a friend you have known since school. Little do you know that you have just set your mate up with a man who is only able to ejaculate if he is watching Jurassic Park.

The only thing worse than being set up with a friend of a friend and it not quite working out is being set up with a member of your friend's family and it not working out.

I am not going to tell you about the chap I was set up with by a friend who tried to get into my knickers by asking to see my 'puss-puss'. Nor am I going to tell you about my friend's mate from school who was an adult bed-wetter. I kind of want to, but I quite like them both – so I will put those experiences in a little box and mark it 'whoops' and move on. I will, however, tell you about Mr Pants. He was my mate's cousin. I call him Mr Pants because of a single picture he once sent me. A picture he took of himself in his pants. It was just of his pants area. They were Y-fronts, to be specific. He thought he was being clever by not putting his face in shot, but the wally had unbelievably recognisable tattoos on show on his arms. It wouldn't have taken Sherlock to put him in the frame.

Anyway. So, what happened with Mr Pants? Well, I don't like to put the blame on others for my decisions. As you know, I am more than happy to put my hands up to being a tit. In this case, though, Mother Nature has to take some responsibility for Mr Pants. To quote Mr William Smith, 'It's like the summer's a natural aphrodisiac'. It was one of those heady summer days normally reserved for Women's Institute summer fete scenes in *Midsomer Murders*. Sadly, Mr Pants didn't look like Bergerac, but on a positive note, nobody died. Well, maybe my dignity, but Mr Dignity has been on borrowed time ever since hooking up with Ms Alcohol at university.

A good friend, Marie, and I were making the most of the beautiful summer's evening by sitting about indoors. Hmm. Well, we had planned to go out but had got distracted discussing why Peter Andre was still famous. Out of the blue, Marie had a text from her cousin:

`'Got any single friends?'`

As he was clearly incredibly choosy, Marie asked me if I would be interested in meeting him for a drink later. She said she hadn't seen him much in recent years, but that she used to spend a lot of time with him growing up and he seemed a nice guy. She showed me a few pictures. I know, I know – but looks are important. I didn't particularly want to meet Sloth from The Goonies. Again.

We wandered down to our local pub with Marie's boyfriend. It was still beautifully hazy. I was feeling on good form. My tan was pretty choco. Admittedly, not from the heady British sun, but from the tanning booths (also known as the £2 human microwaves) near my flat. I don't go anymore. Partly as they are ridiculous due to the skin cancer risks and partly because of the woman on reception. The last time I went in, I wasn't sure if I was speaking to the owner or a talking Shar-Pei dog.

Mr Pants was a lot of fun. Not especially my type, but to be honest the more dates I remember, the less of a type I seem to have. Sometimes I think my type was 'human and single'. Saying that, I had to get on with them, and there was certainly a tick for compatibility here. It was a textbook first 'date'. Lots of laughs, a few vinos and the promise of a pickled egg. There was one thing, though. As the end of the night came upon us, my gaydar starting dinging. Despite the 'touching' and flirting, my glittery gay spidey senses were tingling. So I did what any other person would have done. I took him to a gay club, told him to 'treat himself', and went home.

Oh. You wouldn't have done that?

Interestingly, it was never really mentioned again. Had I known exactly what happened in Spanky Wankys (not the real nightclub name – a genuine shame) then maybe the story would have ended there. Anyway, we started texting. Sometimes a lot, sometimes nothing. He had this charming habit of sending me pictures of himself in the bath. Proper soapy bubble baths enveloping his leg hair. Of course, there was also the infamous pic he sent of just his belly and his M&S underpants. Still, at least he didn't bombard me with knob shots. I had a bad spate of receiving unexpected cock shots from dates. The worst was the video I received from a guy I'd had a single, innocent date with. I was at my desk at work the next morning when 'beep beep' – a message came through. This message was an actual video of him wanking to orgasm. Of course, I did the right thing and deleted it with no comment. Ah, who am I kidding? I passed it around my colleagues and we all marked his technique out of ten. He averaged a four.

I will admit that there was definitely an air of uncertainly around Mr Pants. I couldn't quite place it. We saw each other a few times. I was starting to quite like him. I didn't invest any specifically hardcore feelings, but I felt fuzzy when we spoke. It was all very chaste – well, except for the relatively frequent pictures of his pubes.

The last time I saw him was the time we 'took it further'. We'd been in touch for a few weeks, we'd met up a few times, his cousin was a close mate – what could go wrong? Um. Ok, think of the 'lovemaking scene' from *Ghost*. Then think of the EXACT OPPOSITE. It was over before I knew it had started. Now, that wasn't the issue. The issue was his next actions. He got off me and while he was putting on his trousers told me he 'had to go'. Eh? Now, I knew we weren't love's young dream, and but he didn't even offer me a tissue. That's just rude. Now, I don't want to be graphic here, but I didn't even know where the bloody condom had gone.

    And that was it. After four weeks of texting and pub dates, I never heard from him again. I sure as shit didn't contact him either. I was embarrassed and furious. I had to fork out £26.50 and have an 'interview' for the Morning-After Pill and an STI check. To this day, I have never felt so utterly rank about myself. 'Rank'. Excellent word. I have made some awful decisions, but sleeping with him was award-worthy. That Saturday, he disappeared into the night like Dick Turpin with a semi. He didn't steal my stuff, but he left Mr Dignity gasping for air. It was a true low point.

    The thing is, deep down I did know Mr Pants wasn't for me. I was a bit lonely. Loneliness is often the Keymaster to the Zuul that is bad decisions. Dating is a very lonely game when you keep meeting wankers. Marie felt bloody awful. She literally had no idea that her cousin was such a bell-end. The Fresh Prince of Bell-end in fact. That's a lesson we learnt together. You might know the twelve-year-old, but people can turn into right bastards after puberty. There is a saying: 'show me the boy and I'll show you the man'. I never truly understood it. As soon as wanking comes into play, all bets are off. I decided that I would never take up an offer of a set-up with a friend's family member. Obviously, if my neighbour's uncle was Batman, I might have had a rethink.

So how did love karma bite Mr Pants' hairy bum? A few years later, I was a bridesmaid at my friend's wedding. She was someone that I had met in my new job who I had become close friends with very quickly. During the general post-ceremony chit-chat, I noticed a familiar face. 'Hmm – I recognise that chap,' I thought. Then it clicked. It was Mr Pants. I couldn't believe it. There was no one there whom I had met before, apart from the bride and groom. The bride hadn't even met Marie, so there was no connection there. The look of abject panic on his face was something I hadn't seen before. I asked the bride who he was. She told me:

'Oh, he's my auntie's boyfriend. They have had a bit of an on/off thing going on. To be honest, we don't know why she's with him. I think he might be gay.'

Brilliant.

I decided not to tell her what had happened – it was her wedding day after all. Well, that's not strictly true. I didn't quite tell her the whole story, but I did précis it. She really laughed.

I have never seen anyone look so incredibly uncomfortable for so long. He looked so buttock-clenched, I bet he didn't poo for a week. We did not speak. He did not leave his partner's side. I never worked out whether he had been cheating when he went out with me and that this was the cause of the awkwardness, or whether he was confused about his sexuality, or whether he just knew he had been a total tosser. It didn't matter. It was a beautiful wedding, full of love, and the wedding DJ played "Atmosphere" by Russ Abbot. Twice.

Be careful out there, Love Soldiers. No one ever knows what someone is genuinely like unless they have been out with them. If they are related to them, I would like to believe that wasn't possible. I wouldn't say avoid such situations completely, but I would def advise heading in with a healthy dollop of cynicism. The tale of Mr Pants is another little love karma reminder. Love karma exists, and like the chameleon it is, you'll never know what form it will take. Karma might just be around the corner, dancing to Russ Abbot with your wife.

Short

There was one more set-up before I said, 'Never again'. One Thursday afternoon of nothing special, I got chatting to a colleague. She told me about a mate of hers. He was young(ish), free, single, and in the RAF. She asked if I fancied meeting up with him. Ooh, I thought. RAF. Fancy. Surely if he was in the RAF he was likely to be presentable, eloquent and hopefully not particularly rapey. I genuinely couldn't see what could go wrong. Despite it not being 1980s America, I found myself allowing images of a white-suited Richard Gere to pop into my mind.

    I will add that at no point did my friend insinuate that the Charmer could be long term material. Ok, maybe I didn't understand why just yet. This would become much clearer later on. It was to be casual dating; a 'he's single, you're single, you're both non-ugly – have some fun for a bit' type of thing.

    Admittedly, I shouldn't have ignored the deafening alarm bells that rang out a couple of days before we met. One morning, I woke up to four missed calls and a request for a picture of my lady garden. Bit odd. It was followed by an apologetic email. It read:

`'Sorry, blondie - does one owe one an apology?'`

It seemed like an apology. It seemed sober. It definitely did not show signs of an officer's grammar. Hey ho. It was more than I would have got from Mr Pants or Bodywarmer. I arranged to meet the Charmer one Saturday afternoon. We didn't live too far from each other, so we met on the corner and we wandered down to a nearby uninspiring pub together. He was attractive enough. There was no white aviation suit, but he smelt nice. I did notice that for the whole walk to the pub he was looking at my boobs. I was hard up for attention. I was flattered.

Almost as soon as we got a table and sat down, I knew where he thought it was heading for him. Although I was up for a bit of uncommitted dating, I wasn't sure about being in a bad nineties porn film. He talked about nothing but sex. I played along for a bit, and then, to be honest, I just felt a bit squinky. I tried to get the conversation onto something else. Anything else. The following exchange probably sums him up quite perfectly:

'So, come on then. Tell me a bit about yourself other than your cock. What's your favourite film?'

'Ah ... Shawshank Redemption. Definitely.'

'Everyone says that. What's your real favourite film?'
'Top Gun.'

There wasn't much else to say to that, to be honest, but at least it showed he was capable of a non-sexual thought. Although he did pick the most homoerotic film of all time. Again, it summed him up perfectly. He was so sexual that I started to think he protested too much. And then it happened. Using his feet, he parted my legs under the table. Now – and I cannot stress this enough – this is rapey.

His house was on the way back to mine, and he asked if I wanted to pop in. I know, I know. I am disgusting. I said yes and went round. It was as I was looking at his CDs that he tried to put his finger up my bum. Um, just a side note. If someone is wearing a skirt and leaning over, it's not a specific invitation. If it was, Tesco would be a very different place. Again. Rapey.

The final nail in my 'wondering if this can all be turned about as he's clearly a good guy underneath his balls' coffin was when he referred to his neighbours. They were mutual friends of ours. He asked me if I thought they were 'still at it' – whilst suggestively shoving the scissored fingers of his hands together.

I snogged him anyway.

Look, I never said I made the best judgements at these times. Hell no. This is all about reflection. It's about judging my decisions and actions as much as theirs. If I made the right decision each time, this would be a very short book.

Needless to say, we didn't see each other again.

So, to quote *Under Siege 2*, 'assumption is the mother of all fuck-ups'. Just because he's in the RAF, it doesn't mean he's a gentleman. He could just as easily be a massive pervert.

In fairness, it doesn't necessarily have to be a blind date that throws up the unexpected. You can also have unexpectedly disappointing experiences meeting people who you already know. Well, think you know. Sometimes you inadvertently throw yourself a curve ball. You meet someone in real life. In the flesh. In front of you. Suddenly it feels like Victorian times all over again. Well, if the Victorians met a friend at their house, drank a bottle of Pinot, then headed to a pub in an inappropriately short skirt.

It was a standard Friday evening after work in very similar circumstances that my little anecdote takes place. I'll be honest – pubs after work weren't a regular occurrence for either me or my friend, so we were overexcited.

After an hour or two, the friend I was with met some colleagues and started chatting to them. I say chatting – shouting very loudly and lying on the bench 'for a sleep' was probably closer to the truth, but let's just stick with 'chatting'. I popped to the bar for (let's face it, a hugely ill-advised) fourth or fifth vat of wine.

Then I saw him.

It was like the setting around us melted into 1980s roadhouse bar movie. Sort of like the bar in *The Accused* but without the bit where Jodie Foster gets raped. Anyway, standing propped against the bar was someone who I will calmly describe as a cross between The Rock and Vin Diesel. And then it happened. He looked at me! Meeeeee! After being immersed in the world of internet dating, I had forgotten the tingly pleasure of eyes meeting across a room. We started chatting. Ok, ok. Snogging. Come on, I was in some sexy roadhouse movie with Vin Diesel. We were bound to have a snog.

Last orders were called at the bar and he gave me his card. This hugely impressed me. The last time I had been given a card by a man it had a taxi firm number on it and I was being told I'd 'probably had enough to drink'. He worked for some glamorous computer software company. Brilliant. Sexy, great job, lived in the same city, was interested in me. Check. Check. Check. Check. I could hardly believe it. After all that time trawling through messages on internet dating sites and finding sparks, I'd met this hunk of a man in a pub. Like in the olden days. The Rock and I had one last kiss. Then I woke my friend up from the bench and we went home. I was high on romance and possibility. And probably Chardonnay.

Over the weekend, he popped me a text. He was still interested. Tick! We decided to meet up for a coffee on the Monday at lunchtime. I wangled a long lunch break and went to the Costa (other coffee shops are available but may pay less tax) near my office. I ordered a large Americano. As I sat there with it, a person who can only be described as a sweaty, bald man came in. I didn't think much of it. Then he came over.

I know. You're thinking I am ridiculously shallow. In all fairness, he had the look of someone who was expecting to see Michelle Pfeiffer but Michelle Fowler had turned up. We were both politely disappointed. It turned out that the glamorous computer company was a room with his mate where they adjusted software. Nope, still not sure what that means. Man, it was painful. I really, really tried. He had nothing to say. I then realised. We hadn't talked in the bar. At all. My tongue being in his mouth for the majority of the time I had known him had probably prevented conversation. Argh! All I could think was: why had I ordered such a sodding massive coffee?

Note to self. In the future, always order espresso.

We said our goodbyes and I almost ran back to work (that illustrates in itself how buttock-clenching it was). There and then, I decided not to be so harsh on internet dating. You get to chat, see what shared interests you have, and be open about what you want and what you're looking for. Ok, you might see the odd misleading profile picture, but there is one thing that will always be far more misleading. Wine.

At least I wasn't disappointed. He was a stranger to me and absolutely no specific romantic dreams had been dashed by meeting him. It's another cliché, but generally, it feels better to have a bash at something and for it not to work out than to regret not having a bash at it at all. My sister was always especially fab at encouraging me to just go for it. As long as I was safe and was not meeting strangers for tit-wanks in pub toilets, then there was no reason not to rip the plaster off and meet someone. Being in the modern world we call twenty-first century Britain, dating opportunities can arise in places where you least expect them. In places like Australia, social media sites such as Facebook are a common place for hooking up with friends of friends. It isn't nicknamed Fuckbook for nothing. In Britain, things are a bit more demur. We genuinely do mainly use it to keep in touch with school friends and to passively stalk exes, occasionally checking out how fat their new girlfriends are. So when a work colleague of a friend of mine started messaging me out of the blue, I found it all a bit alien, but, not being one to pass up an opportunity for male attention, I replied. Soon we were chatting. He was a colleague of my friends'. He was Italian, divorced, charming. I hadn't come across many Italian men. I associated them all with Super Mario. Mr Italian knew what to say to get my attention and I really enjoyed chatting with him. He lived in London and asked if I was ever in the city. Well, actually I was. It was an easy plan. My sister could do a bit of babysitting while I popped out for wine by the Thames.

I wavered fairly heavily over this one. It being in London added to my feelings of insecurity. If we didn't like each other, at best I would be stuck with some Dilbert, a long way from home comforts. At worst, I would be dredged from the Thames, piece by piece. My sister quite rightly told me I was being a donut. She assured me that she would be 'on call' and close by and told me to just go for it. So I did.

It was raining, dreary and dark. I stood nervously by Covent Garden Tube station trying not to look like I was there to do favours for sailors. In the distance, I saw a familiar face. He just wasn't quite as far away from me as I had first thought he was – he was THAT short. Honestly, I am not that bothered about people looking a certain way. I would probably prefer a chubby over a skinny, but I have dated all sorts. Saying that, there is chubby and then there is sweaty fat-fat. I went on a few dates with a journalist, and he was sweaty fat. On our third date, I remember looking at his t-shirt. It had started to ride up, exposing a couple of inches of white, hairy flesh. It glistened with sweat. I looked up to notice rings of darkened, sweat-soaked t-shirt under his armpits. Ugh. Luckily, he was also a self-obsessed twat bucket so I didn't worry about not wanting to see him again.

Height, on the other hand, had never been an issue. I tended to head for taller chaps, Jim had been shorter than me and I wasn't bothered. We're all the same height lying down and all that. Man, though – Mr Italian did throw me. He didn't even reach my shoulder.

He was absolutely charming and it wasn't long before I didn't notice the height. We sat on a terrace and had wine. He was a bit intense. When I say that he looked me in the eye, I mean that he bored through me with his pupils as we sat together sharing a drink. It probably would have been fine had it not started raining. We went on to find a seat inside but it was standing room only. It is tough trying to pretend not to notice the person you are on a date with is almost a foot shorter than you. If we'd known each other better, we could have cracked a joke or two. Still, I was willing to give it a bash. I slipped off my heels and things looked a bit less comical. That was until he asked to smell my neck. I said that was fine. Big mistake. He would not stop smelling me. Big, strong, earthy breaths. Without my heels on, I was just about the right height for him to nuzzle into my neck. Maybe it was the Gucci Envy. Maybe it was the wine. Maybe he was a sex pest. Whatever the reason, he could not get enough of my neck.

Still, you know me. I was on the vino, too, and after a while it started not to seem so strange – although there was one moment when he took in another earthy breath and I looked up to see a chap who used to be in *Brookside* visibly shuddering at the sight of Mr Italian straining to get closer to the pheromones by my earlobes. Weird.

I wasn't sure what was happening between us. I had no idea if I liked him or if I was in the Dating Twilight Zone. It got nearer the witching hour that was pub closing time and I made my excuses to head for the Tube. Mr Italian wanted to accompany me to my train, which I thought was romantic. Outside the station, he beckoned me towards him and kissed me. Actually, that was good – a little uncomfortable, but he had a beautiful way of kissing. A few moments later, we were interrupted by a chap walking past. He tapped Mr Italian on the shoulder and we broke our embrace. The chap walking past then proceeded to ask Mr Italian if he wanted a Cornetto and tried to shove one in his face. Were we being mugged with an ice cream? Who knows. Luckily, the ice cream man left us to it. Seamlessly, my Italian blindsided the incident by asking me if I wanted to get a room.

I declined and headed for the Northern line, not quite believing what had just happened.

I guess the lesson in Mr Italian is to just give it a bash. If things aren't quite what you were hoping for, at the very least you are likely to get a decent anecdote out of it. It was also a lesson for me to remember that meeting someone online can be a bit of a Forrest Gump – you never know what you're gonna get. The more open-minded you are about the soft centres, the more likely you are to meet that decent someone. And you know what? Every disappointing toffee penny brings the potential to give a dentist the chance to make a few quid replacing a filling.

Sometimes you can know someone fairly well and still be surprised by them. Well, as you may remember I have mentioned before about dipping your pen in the office ink. I confess that I did not learn my lessons with Tom.

The Hobbit wasn't a relationship at all. I met the Hobbit at my next job. I was a PA. I was a crap PA. I wasn't very organised and most people got on my tits. Still, I hid it fairly well and got on with the chocolate teapot tasks I was assigned. My boss was a heavy smoker, yet insisted on £250+ a night rooms. If you've ever tried to find a smoking room in a swanky place, you'll understand. Unless you're a generic sixties rock star and can afford the redecoration costs, it's impossible. Still, to quote my boss (adopt broad Glaswegian accent):

'Aaaaam the mooost eeeasyygoin' bloooke in the worlyd.'

He bloody wasn't.

Sorry, again I digress.

I was also assigned to the Hobbit to help him out with basic PA duties. It was an odd set-up. I hadn't met him in person, and all the work was done over the phone. The moment I realised we would get on was when I had to book his first hotel. He had to stay in a dilapidated seaside town which was central to a business that our company wanted to buy. I searched and searched hotels and B&Bs on TripAdvisor. I relayed all the reviews back to him to see which he thought would be the least offensive to stay in. The most memorable review was one that stated simply: 'Mattress. Soiled.'

I booked him into a hotel in the neighbouring city.

Over the following months, I began to get to know him. We had a similar sense of humour, and chatting to him was the perfect antidote to 'the most easy-going bloke in the world', i.e. my anally retentive boss.

When I met him, I was baffled. He was the epitome of 'not what I expected'. Five foot nothing, tanned and sporting what looked like macaroni jewellery (later this was confirmed to be a leather necklace, but to be honest, potayto/potahto). It was a massive lesson for me. I started to understand that the saying 'looks aren't that important' was not just a made-up statement to make ugly people and fatties feel better. I had got to know the Hobbit blind, and I had to admit that I had a little crush on him.

Two years into my job, I was made redundant. Well, I say *I* was. Actually, my boss was. Nobody actually told me. Um, the thing is, when you're a PA and your boss gets made redundant, you really should have a word with HR. So that was it. My official last day was the 24th December (Haaappy Chriiiistmas to meeee!). I was sad because I'd made some great friends there. The job was shite, though. Still, they gave me a tidy sum and a shining reference.

On my last day, my closest colleague friends, including the Hobbit, came along for drinky fun. The night was marred slightly by my choice of outfit. There is nothing sexy or dignified about trying to get yourself back into a tight hotpants jumpsuit after two bottles of Pinot. Especially when the zip breaks and you're not wearing a bra. (The colleague who got me back from the brink of an unintentional streak home is still a friend. I thank you.)

Late in the evening, I got chatting with the Hobbit. We did some kissing. I don't remember how it happened, but it did. It was great. I felt like I was at school and had just got together with the boy in my maths class that I'd fancied for

years. Saying that, I went to an all-girls' school, so it's not the best analogy. You get what I mean. I popped to the loo and a friend asked me how things were going. When I told her, she was surprised. I'll never forget this. She said:
'Ah, right. I wasn't sure if you were kissing or just leaning on his head.'

She had a point. I was probably around 5ft 11 in my heels. We looked like The Krankies, only he was Wee Jimmy. Nevertheless, the Hobbit and I went back to mine for a bit more kissing. Lovely job.

Now I won't go into too much detail, but it's fair to say that I got to test whether we really are 'all the same height lying down'. It was just when things were about to get particularly interesting that he sat bolt upright and said suddenly – as if he had just remembered:
'I can't do this. I have a girlfriend. She's lovely.'
'Eh?'

Now, this wasn't the first time this had happened to me. When I was at university, I had done some kissing in my room with a friend's mate at one of our house parties. He had the gall to get a bit naked before telling me he had a girlfriend. So I scratched his back. No, I mean I reeeeeally scratched his back up. I remember him getting up, seeing his back in the mirror, panicking and asking me if I thought it looked like a rugby injury. It didn't.

I wasn't going to be so cruel to the Hobbit. I'd known him for nearly two years. Ok, there was a part of me that hoped he would get strangled by his own home-made necklace, but I wasn't going to behave like a scorned puppy. I took it for what it was. I liked him more than he liked me, and he had just hurt my feelings. Pure and simple, as the song goes. I didn't blame myself, as I'd had no idea he had a girlfriend. That was his problem. If he could tell himself that by not getting his willy out, he wasn't cheating, then great for him. For the record, I believe any exchange of bodily fluid is probably cheating. Maybe I'm just terribly old-fashioned.

As it was technically my leaving do, I didn't have to see him again. But it was a reminder of the importance of just how sure you need to be if you're going to start messing about with a colleague's stationery. A more positive lesson I learnt from my Lord of the Rings experience, however, was not to be so picky when it comes to looks. Before I knew the Hobbit, I had thought that height was imperative – but it isn't. I realised that as soon as you release yourself from having a 'type', the world of dating opens up a little more. Unless you are happy being alone for a touch longer than you are comfortable with, I wouldn't advise restricting your search for love to rigid guidelines. When I say 'rigid', I mean it's ok to stick to looking for someone who has a job or who doesn't pick their nose and wipe it on you. Just try not to be too blinkered. In the words of the modern theorist Joey Tribbiani:[5] 'There's lots of flavours out there. Grab a spoon.'

---

[5] As seen in the nineties sitcom *Friends*. If you don't know who I am talking about,
I am surprised you are someone who has read this much of my book.

Drugs

So there I was, grabbing scoops and testing all the flavours out there whilst carefully trying to avoid the tutti-frutti. I say 'testing', as my dance card was fairly clear. I was just at the 'starter message' stage of the internet dating search. I hadn't been inspired enough to meet anyone for a while.

It's funny how quickly that can change. One rainy Sunday evening, I was scrolling through the messages I had received over the weekend. I had recently signed up to match.co.uk. No, I meant .co.uk. It was an el cheapo version of the better-known site match.com. In hindsight, this was my first clue as to the clientele. There was the usual uninspired collection of messages that just said 'hey' and a few other dull comments. Then a little note caught my eye. It referenced what I had written on my profile, which was always nice. But more than that, he just looked fun. In the background of his profile picture, he was relaxing in a park, and I could see he had rested a can of Red Stripe in a Reebok. It's funny that my first reaction was 'Ooh, fun' when it could just as easily have been 'Ooh, he looks like a borderline alcoholic'.

Frank Squarehead didn't live in the same city as me, but I thought he was perky, and there was something about him that made me want to get to know him a little better. After a week or so of chit-chatting and texting, he drove up and met me for lunch. He had the sweetest car – a vintage red Audi (if a fifteen-year-old car is vintage), and I thought it was marvellous. Well, I did until he told me he called it Christine. Christine was the name of a car possessed by a vengeful spirit in a Stephen King novel. Hmm.

The day was simple enough. He met me in a coffee shop and then we went on to lunch. It was a fun few hours. He didn't 'forget his wallet', and there was no leg-parting under the table, no false teeth, no bum-picking, and no vegetarianism. Not that I have issues with vegetarians, but ever since Paul they make me a bit nervy on the manliness scale.

So all was good with Frank. He was tall, dark and handsome and as soon as we realised that we both loved Chevy Chase, I knew I wanted to see him again. I walked him to his car and before he got in, he leant forward and kissed me. And we clashed teeth. There is no get-out for a tooth clash. The moment was well and truly ruined. Who knows why or how that happened, being the seasoned kisser that I am. Perhaps evil Christine was jealous.

Despite the bad kiss, we continued to tick along nicely. We didn't rush into anything. It was a bonus that he didn't live too close by, as it meant that we got to know each other over emails, texts and calls. He worked in a hospital, and that massively impressed me. If I am being honest, it took me back to when I was eleven and would Tipp-Ex 'Casualty' on my pencil case because I fancied Julian Chapman (Google 'Nigel Le Vaillant'. Yes, I still 'would'). He would send me bits and pieces. The blood-splatter masks were a favourite. The Christmas tree at work was decorated in blown-up sanitising gloves. Admittedly, though, nothing he sent could ever beat the time a nurse friend of mine brought me a vaginal clamp as a gift to a barbecue. We used it to serve the salad.

One evening, he wanted to send a couple of pictures to my phone. Now, you should understand that this was six years ago – there was no iPhone or wireless broadband for me back then. The pictures wouldn't load on my piece-of-shit Motorola mobile, but as luck would have it, my mate Lisa was over. Knowing that he wouldn't send them to her phone, I told him I had a work phone and to send them to that number. Which he did. A few days later, I had a near-hysterical (laughing, not panic) call from my friend who that day had received a short series of nipple and stomach pube shots of a chap she had never met. Clearly, he thought I would like to see a little more.

Things started to go quite well between us. We started to see each other about once a week. We had proper 'dates' too. We once went ice-skating – one of the many, many things I am shite at.[6] It would've been polite if he'd told me he grew up in Canada. Sometimes people genuinely do not believe I am as bad at things as I say I am. Years ago, when I went on a date which involved bowling, the guy I was with got genuinely agitated and accused me of being shit on purpose. Frank, however, was very sweet about it and loyally helped me limp about the ice. From a distance, we looked like an unshaven Christopher Dean trying to stop a blond Forrest Gump in his leg braces from breaking his face.

We lived around a hundred miles apart, but it didn't seem to matter too much. When he drove to visit me, we had a deal that as he had to pay for travel, I would pay for food and drink while he was with me. Now, that sounds fairly innocuous – but boy, could he drink. Now, I can drink. Believe me, I am not shy about sloshing vino into my wine glass. But he was something else. One visit, he opened a

---

[6] The list also includes: water-skiing; tenpin bowling; windsurfing; roller skating; running for more than fifteen minutes; and coping without wine for longer than a week

bottle of wine at 11.30am and drank continuously through the afternoon, getting through four bottles and the *National Lampoon* box set. It wasn't a great thing for my dwindling bank balance.

Things ticked along fabulously for a few months. Everything just seemed right. The only hitch we seemed to come across was when I noticed he wore fingerless gloves and I called him Fagin. He didn't find it funny.

One visit, out of the blue, he asked what I thought about the idea of us living together. The idea of moving didn't faze him one bit. He said that as he worked as a locum already, he could easily find work up near where I lived. It was overwhelming. The bloody birds sang in my head. Flamingos bowed in the lakes. After four years in the dating wilderness, had I done it? Was it the end of four long years of dating without making any headway? This was it. The One. Wasn't it? Well, truth be known, I wasn't sure about the 'forever' tag – but I was definitely pleased as Punch to consider him The Significant Someone for a while.

That weekend, our goodbye felt especially sad. He didn't want to go. I didn't want him to go. He told me he loved me, and I said it back. I thought I was in love. Had we not been standing outside our city's equivalent of Del Boy's Nelson Mandela House, it would have been beautifully romantic. It's funny, really. I have been in love four times.

Well, I thought I was, at those times. Truthfully, it's just been the once, with a possible fleeting twice – and that most certainly wasn't Frank. I couldn't know that, though, because it was only when I fell in love in 2010 that I realised what True Love was. Anyway, I am jumping ahead. Plus, I am starting to sound like a bit of a wanker.

That Monday, I tootled off to work happily. We had a few cheeky texts. All was marvellous in the bucket that was Frank and I. That evening he said he was off round to his mate's house to smoke and listen to some Northern Soul. I didn't think much of it. I didn't hear from him that evening. The next morning came and went, and I still hadn't heard from him. The next evening passed by and still there was nothing from Frank. Finally, on Wednesday, two days after I had last heard from him, I received a text from him. I can't quite remember all of it, but I do remember it ended with:

`'Sometimes I think ur not right for me.'`

I felt sick. I had no idea where the hell it had come from. Only that Sunday we had been together, and he (HE!!!) had asked about us living together and had gone through how it was possible. I threw together a response along the lines of 'our differences are what makes us so great' or some bollocks.

He never replied.

That literally was it. Nothing. I was devastated. He dumped me out of the blue, put the responsibility on me, and gave me no right to reply. It was torture. Was I so piss-awful that you could be in love with me one day, bugger off to your own house, and then realise that I was so utterly hideous that you couldn't even bear to reply to a sodding text message?

    I did try and call him. Just once. My friend who had endured the pube pics also tried to call him. Just once. But that's it. I am proud of that. I did consider waiting another four months and then asking him if he wanted to meet his new son. But I didn't.

    It wasn't long before I woke up and fully appreciated how very wrong he was for me. I used to think he looked sexy in the bath. Really, it was because it forced his stupid hair off his face. If we'd stayed together, I would've been bankrupt in a year, as I sodding paid for everything – plus my liver would have signed me up for a transplant of its own accord. He stole shitloads from the NHS, and I am also fairly sure he was a habitual drug user, but I just didn't want to see it at the time. I remember going through it all with Mum. When I asked her if she thought he still did drugs, she responded:

'Well, he was terribly thin.'

    Oh.

The bottom line is that someone who can make you believe they love you and can then break your heart without an ounce of cushioning is just not a very nice person. Cushioning is so important. Sometimes a sprinkle of 'It's not you, it's me' is all it takes. If you simply must dump by text, please respond. Even if it really is them, and they are psychotic to the point of needing medical assistance, just say that it's your issues, not theirs. There is a special place in the anus of hell that waits for those who mess about with love without at least attempting to protect the love-afflicted person from more hurt than is necessary.

I had been dumped – out of the blue and two weeks before Christmas. I will freely admit that I spent the next few days in tears, although if I was being honest with myself, it wasn't about 'losing' Frank. It was more that the text he had sent had laid the blame at my feet. Saying 'sometimes I think you're not right for me' made me feel that there was something fundamentally wrong with me; that I was the issue. The notion that I was never ever going to be able to make anyone happy in a relationship hung in the air like one of those farts people do that make you want to ask them if they need to go to the toilet.

The turning point came fairly quickly. Just a few days after getting 'that' text, I picked up a parcel from the post room. I opened it. I can tell you now that nothing twists the already protruding knife in your back so nicely than when four days later the gift you have sought and bought them arrives. Hmm. Hey ho, though. I realised then that I had invested far too much in him. If he could be so cruel to someone that he had appeared to care for so much, then he just wasn't worth any more self-pity. It was the slap I needed. I vowed there and then to save the gift for someone I knew would appreciate it. As it happens, that didn't happen until seven years later. I was able to send it to a friend for their birthday – a friend I had known for a few years through my sister, and someone who understood the pleasure that only an original 1970s vinyl recording of *Monty Python Live at the Hollywood Bowl* could give.

Funnily enough, the other day I was doing a bit of furniture rearranging in the living room. After we had been seeing each other a few weeks, Frank had bought me a beautiful canvas photographic print of Marilyn Monroe. I had kept it up in the hallway. I loved it and still do. After moving things around a little, I now had a spot for it on the wall of my living room. As I moved it from the hall, I noticed the note he had written on the back:

'To one misfit from another.'

Me? Misfit?

Fuck off.

After Frank, I allowed myself a four-day binge of tears and menthol cigs, but that was all. I decided that the motherfucker had no right to steal my love faith and, more pressingly, my Christmas. Without thinking too hard about it, I got straight back on the horse that was more commonly known to me as plentyoffish.com. I refused to let someone so cruel rob me of the self-esteem that I had clawed back after everything that happened years before.

I also had a little boost from an unlikely source. I like to listen to a bit of Radio 2 in the car. One morning, not long after Frank had unceremoniously dumped me, a song came on the radio. It was the Bublé singing 'Haven't Met You Yet'. If you haven't heard it, or you need a reminder, download it. It is an uplifting song. The lyrics simple, the song catchy. It made such a massive difference from all the maudlin slow drivel about love lost and being shafted. Instead, it focused on the future. You know what, Olwen? He might still be out there waiting meet you.

With that ditty in my heart, I forged ahead towards the new year. What's that saying? 'The best way to get over someone is to get under someone else.' Well, ok, I am not sure I entirely agree with that. I don't know of many relationships that have blossomed from a desperate and urgent need for immediate flattery and reassurance. Still, if you are sure that the other person is attracted to you and at least wants to see your boobs, it can act as a nice little plaster to get you through a break-up.

My advice on that front would be to head back to a place and time when you felt most secure and seek out something along those lines. For some people, it means sending a flirtatious message to an old school flame you know always fancied you. Me? Well, that was easy. Back to the military.

Almost immediately, I got chatting to a soldier who was on leave. He was beautiful, fun, sexy and completely inappropriate for long-term consideration. Even better, it was just chit-chat until after Christmas. Really, it wasn't even all that sexual. The basis of our discussions were the Guinness World Record attempts I had introduced at work, namely the Ferrero Rocher Challenge.[7] It acted as a nice little bit of superglue for my confidence, which had been smashed to pieces a few days before. We met up just the once. It was after Christmas, before he went back to Ireland. We had a cracking night and he helped me keep my head above the dating waters and forge ahead to the new year.

---

[7] Eating as many Ferrero Rocher chocs as you can in a minute. I managed just under six. The female office champion. Proud moment.

Thick

'Three, two, one ... Happy New Year!'

New Year's Eve that year was one of my favourites. It was just me and two best mates in my living room. By some miracle, the three of us found ourselves alone with no plans on that night. Their respective partners had made their own plans and I had none. It was a perfect night of TV karaoke, vino and wondering how we all got to be nearly thirty. It was the perfect end to teen/twenties New Year's Eves.

January dawned, and along with the new year, my desire to look for love diminished. It wasn't that I had given up; it was more that I just wasn't interested in taking the risks anymore. I needed a break. Still, you know what they say about when you stop looking.

I passively kept an eye on plentyoffish.com. There was one chap that I couldn't quite ignore. I know that I have told you all about my Arnold Schwarzenegger thing. If we are all honest, each and every one of us has a sneaky fantasy romantic scenario in our heads – the fantasy ideal that we hope one day might come to fruition. Well, I hoped that one day I would meet some ridiculously hunky man and we would have a very loving, disjointed relationship based pretty much on me feeding him mince and the two of us having wild sex in between his gym sessions. He would be from somewhere in Europe. Germany preferably, or Holland. Maybe Austria. Ah, yes. An Austrian. I would teach him English and in return, he would pick up a lot of heavy barrels and chop wood. Yes, I know, I seem to be back on the subject of Arnold again. Arnie in *Commando*, more specifically. Saying that, Arnie in *True Lies*. Yes, dinner jacket Arnie in *True Lies*. Sexy stuff.

Anyway.

Late one evening, I was doing as many singles do – sitting comfy with a vino and flicking through the messages I had received on plentyoffish.com. I normally did well for messages. (Truth be known, you could sort of see my left nipple in my profile pic.) I tended to ignore the messages that just said 'Hi'. My theory was that if you could only muster the energy to type two letters, you probably wouldn't be able to keep up with me. One exception, however, was Thick Bernie. (This is not even close to his real name, but it doesn't half illustrate him.) You see, he didn't say much in his message – but ooh, he was burly. Even better than that, he looked a bit like Bernard Bresslaw. Suddenly, my little fantasy romance flicked across my eyes.

Who is Bernard Bresslaw, you ask? Ah, he is my *Carry On* fave. No one could 'corrr' like Bernard. I quite liked the idea of being looked after by big, muscly, cockney Bernard. With that fantasy in mind, I got chatting to Thick Bernie.

When I met him, I wasn't disappointed. He was much burlier than I had even dared to wish for, with just the right number of tattoos. Not that I normally gravitate towards biker chic, but c'mon – a big, muscly man with some inking is nice. After all, with the disaster of Frank still hanging in the back of my mind, Thick Bernie was a hunky breath of fresh air.

Ok, so Thick Bernie was from Suffolk and so was not quite the lederhosen-trimmed package I'd been picturing, but his local dialect was just about heavy enough to be considered a language barrier. Although it was nothing compared to when I went out with Jim, who was a Geordie. I only understood around 65% of what Jim said – and that was on a good day.

Charming as he was, Thick Bernie and I were never going to set the world on fire with our lively discussion. It wasn't long before I realised that he probably had his daughter's name tattooed on him so that he could remember how to spell it. In all fairness, there were times when he questioned my intelligence, too. I distinctly remember one exchange when he was telling me about his last night out:

'I was out with Irish Pat.'

'Ah, Irish Pat! Great nickname.'

'Well, we call him that 'cause he's Irish and he's called Pat.'

Hmm.

Now, I don't profess to be particularly sophisticated. Whilst I will happily sup caviar from the back of a maiden's warm hand, I am just as happy with a three-piece meal from AFC. (That's American Fried Chicken to you. Nothing at all to do with KFC. No similarities.) Still, when Bernie praised my Italian food as 'a bit better than the Tesco ready meal one I had' and then asked for ketchup, I wasn't sure we were in exactly the same ballpark.

I wasn't sure about him, so I enlisted the help of a good friend. We were having a mini-party for the twenty-fifth anniversary live episode of *EastEnders*. Oh yes! That's how I roll, baby. It wasn't so much the reveal of the killer we were interested in. More the potential screw-ups. This was a few years before the infamous 'How's Adam?' from Tanya, but Jack Branning – a.k.a. 'the missing link' – fluffed his lines, and that was good enough.

I thought this would be a good, relaxed time to get an opinion on Thick Bernie, so I invited him over, too. Now, let this be a word of warning to all those of you with a very close, protective friend who has seen you have a load of crappy dates. Lisa did not go easy on him. Poor Thick Bernie may as well have had Lisa sitting backwards on a plastic chair and pointing a light in his face. I believe she used the phrase: 'And if you hurt her, you will have me to answer to...'.

If I am being honest, I was completely touched by the care of my mate and also quite impressed by how well Thick Bernie handled it. After the reel of questions, every one of which he answered, he simply sat back, sighed, and said: 'Blimey, for a minute there I thought I'd killed Archie.'

When he went home, I asked my mate what she thought about him. She simply said: 'Olwen, he seems like a nice guy and you obviously like each other but (and she looked at me when she said this) ... really?'

The next (and as it happens, final) time we met brought the real nail in the coffin of our alliance. It was an innocent conversation about celebrities that we fancied. When I posed the question, he enthusiastically told me his top woman was Cheryl Cole. And that was that. I couldn't continue to date someone whose top fantasy woman was Cheryl Cole. I am ok with anyone wanting to do her over a canoe after a few cans of Stella, but I could never have a long-term relationship with someone who held Cheryl Cole as their top woman. She is serving drinks on The Plane,* for goodness' sake.

*The Plane. I conceptualised The Plane to describe anyone who gets on your tits. It's a fantasy plane that will eventually disappear to an island where its passengers can stay and breed at will with their own kind. If any of my friends find someone annoying, they will text me and request a ticket for The Plane so that they can mentally put the person on it. It is purely for famous people – not for anyone we know. Standard irritating celebs are passengers; the painfully irritating have jobs. Providing he can stop singing sodding Mysterious Girl to the elderly for five minutes, Peter Andre is the pilot. Don't get me wrong. All of the judgments for The Plane are completely unfounded and more than likely completely unfair. If I was to actually know any of the 'passengers' I have no doubt that I would be charmed and feel dreadful about the whole thing. I'm sure that should I ever be lucky enough to meet Christian Bale, he would have removed that massive pole from up his arse and would be in fact be incredibly charismatic. Until then, he is checking passports at The Plane terminal.

I digress massively, but you get the idea.

You would think I would be able to explain why Cheryl Cole was a particularly bad choice, but I can't. Logic doesn't come into it. It's just a thing. Ok, a conviction for assault that's seemingly been forgotten whilst we are all told that she's 'the nation's sweetheart' doesn't help.

Sorry. Back to Thick Bernie.

Later that particular evening, I started to clam up. Ironically, although we had dated for a couple of months under the guise of a fantasy relationship, we had never had sex. There had been lots of kissing and fun, but I just wasn't ever 'ready' for naked penis action with him. It was like there was some sort of physical block I had. I had no idea whether it was because, after everything that had happened with Frank, I just couldn't let go. Ok, so I'd had a brief little fling with the army soldier in between, but this was different. This was nakedness with a vulnerability that came with truly getting to know someone and more importantly letting them get to know me. Considering this was supposedly to be a sexy fantasy romance, I knew something was seriously wrong.

Knowing in my heart that even if David Hasselhoff had hoisted himself around my shoulders and sung 'Looking for Freedom',[8] the wall I had built up between Thick Bernie and me was never going to be knocked down. That was the end of that. I told him that I wasn't over my ex and that 'we'

---

[8] David Hasselhoff had a key role in bringing down the Berlin Wall. Honestly – look it up. Well, when I say 'key role', he had an incredible keyboard scarf and a rousing tune

weren't going to go any further. On reflection, I do wonder if there was an element of truth in that. I didn't know what was going on. To be honest, I didn't need to say it. He knew that things weren't heading in the direction of love.

Ultimately, my fantasy relationship was just a fool's paradise. Although I probably would have thought the same regardless of who it had been with – at that point, I was done with the whole thing. I was genuinely fed up with my search for love. I had no idea whether it was what happened with Frank that really knocked the last few nails into the coffin of my hopes, but after Thick Bernie I felt as if the whole thing was over for me. It was as though the concept of love in its truest form seemed like a fantasy in itself.

After Bernie, my belief was really starting to wane. He was a sweet, attractive guy, but I felt nothing for him. I didn't know whether it was the lack of connection or whether it was just me. Had my ability to fall in love been well and truly smooshed by Pete? Maybe so, and maybe Frank did the final slam dunk.

You know, had it not been for the unexpected message exchange from the chap clutching a pack of Marlboro Lights in his photo, I probably would have given up sooner. There was something about our exchanges. This chap was different. I found myself falling for the lure of a

potential love interest one more time. I didn't rush into it. We talked for two weeks before I found myself agreeing to meet him for that pub quiz. Then I got that text. The text that slammed the final nail into the coffin containing my hopes and dreams of love:
`'I'm sorry, it's not you, it's me. I just can't meet you'.`

There it was. I finally had my evidence that love and romance was all bollocks. Even if it wasn't bollocks in its entirety, it certainly was with regard to any long-term capacity. Anything that feels like love will fall to shit because one person cares more than the other. People will always wonder if there is anything better out there for them. After a year or two, people start to be less and less bothered about seeing the same person naked over and over again. Then there are some people who see a spark with someone but can't even face getting out of the house to meet them in person because they know feelings don't last forever.

I kept a profile going on the website, but my heart was well and truly not in it. It felt like I was wading through treacle – going nowhere, and with fewer and fewer possibilities to get out of my loveless rut. A few days after I had my cancellations from Mr Marlboro Lights, I agreed to go on a date with another chap who seemed ok. We didn't seem to have much in common and the banter felt a little forced, but he was attractive and interested. He suggested he was in police security, which appealed to me. To be honest, at this time I just needed someone to be willing to leave the house to come and see me.

On the night I should have been meeting Mr Marlboro for the pub quiz, I found myself down at my local dating spot meeting a guy I didn't really feel anything for. Not even excitement. It's funny how even through email messages you can know there is no interest. When I saw him, he looked like he could have been a friend of my dad's. He was a late-middle-aged chap and he was wearing a beige Aertex. I could see his man nipples. We sat down and he started to talk. And talk. And talk. He talked about himself. There was not an inkling of interest about what my thoughts were and what I was about. Nothing. It also became clear he was in 'private security'. Most definitely not the same as the police.

Eventually, I made my excuses and said I needed to get home. At that point, he did get a bit more animated. I had forgotten, but he had been on a trip away and I had jokingly asked for a gift from the airport. Sadly, his execution of the joke just made him sound a bit rapey. He became blind to his own insistence as he pressed me repeatedly to go to his car so he could 'show me his Toblerone'. I ran out of the back door. I got home, flaked on the sofa and officially gave up.

When I say gave up, I didn't shut myself off in a hole, but I did mute my expectations. What did I know, anyway? I mean, I had spent my whole life on a vague search for what I thought love was and should be. I realised that it was likely to be all bollocks. I had had the teenage love that couldn't be sustained, the threatening love that nearly broke me, and I had been let down by promises of love. I was nearly thirty, and all of my experiences of love had ended in either disappointment or disaster. I had reached the stage that I didn't even know what I was looking for anymore. Did it even exist?

It was then that I realised. Love wasn't a plot in a TV show. It was never going to be the 1980s / *Neighbours* / Scott and Charlene all-encompassing romance. Love in musicals is idealistic. But real life wasn't a Gene Kelly tap routine.

It's odd that after everything that had happened in my early twenties, it was not until I was nearly thirty that I had the revelation that what I'd been looking for probably never existed in the first place. I understood maternal love. I considered again if that was all I wanted. Perhaps the love that I had been looking for over the past few years had been there all along, staring at me through the eyes of my daughter. She was all the love I needed.

I didn't call off the search. It was more like I was putting it in a little box. I decided to view it in the way that some people view other dreams; they might promise themselves that they'll go and see the pyramids one day, for example. They probably won't, but it's nice to believe the dream might be there waiting when they get around to it.

Perhaps the search for that all-encompassing love was only ever going to end with an emptiness. It was a relief. A genuine relief that I didn't have to keep looking for an ideal, but that in fact it was perfectly fine to meet a nice chap, have some interests in common, find each other attractive and be happy in each other's company.

Fairy Tale?

I was finally completely out of the dating loop. And you know what? It was lovely. Instead of spending the evenings when Jessica was with her father building myself up to meet some bloke, only for the night to end in disappointment, I started to concentrate on myself. I joined Lovefilm and got through all of the films I had always wanted to see but had never got round to watching, classics such as *One Flew Over the Cuckoo's Nest* and *Deliverance*. Unsurprisingly, I kept well and truly clear of any romantic films. If I did venture out, it was far more likely to be with Lisa and Helen, and I avoided all typically heterosexual-male-dominated venues. The Castle became my venue of choice, and in many ways, it was the place that helped me get a bit of control back. I dug out my lesbian tendencies and met women for kisses, and I danced with some of the most fabulous gay men you could ever wish to meet. It was so liberating to be able to approach someone without the fear of rejection. It was a safe place that took me back to the hedonistic time when I was seventeen and discovering myself for the first time. Yes, I know how wanky that sounds, but nevertheless, it is true.

Of course, it could never have just ended there for me. It was a few months later, just after my second favourite time of the year, that I felt better and ready to put myself out there again. Eurovision always manages to ignite the excited optimist in me. So there I was again, with a blank profile page in front of me which needed my enthusiasm. In many ways, I felt like I was truly starting again. I sat blank-faced in front of the screen. Where on Earth do I start? I found myself filling out a plentyoffish.com profile. Easy enough. At the time, it involved no financial outlay so it felt fairly risk-free. I popped down the usual pictures and quirky comments and sat back to see who was out there. Perhaps not in the same blinkered, optimistic way as before I met Frank. I didn't think I ever could be that way again. Still, I was optimistic nevertheless.

It wasn't long before I was exchanging messages with a pleasant enough chap. He was handsome and had a particularly cheeky sense of humour. He was wearing a bodywarmer in his main profile picture. I know – after the Bodywarmer, you would have thought I wouldn't want to go anywhere near him and would label him a 'posh twat'. But for some reason, with him, I couldn't get the image of

Michael J. Fox out of my head. Thank you, *Back to the Future*. His messages were funny and flattering. He was settled and had his own house and a job. There were no weird, out-of-the-blue sexual propositions. I felt oddly comfortable.

After a week of messages and a few text messages, he was keen to chat on the phone. I was happy with that. He just liked me and wanted to chat and get to know me a little better in person. It made such a huge change for someone to be honest and up front about his feelings and his reason for wanting to speak on the phone – and for it not to be so he could try and wank off to the sound of my breathing.

The first time he called me, we talked for two hours. It was fab. He was really funny. It's not unusual for me to come across as a bit harsh with my humour when it comes to potential partners. It's probably a bit of a test mixed with a defence mechanism. He took it all really well and gave as good as he got without making me want to cry. I learnt about him and what he was looking for and in turn I found myself opening up. He knew that my faith and expectations were pretty low and he was keen to change my opinion. He was clear and caring and told me that I needed to just be willing to take another risk with my feelings and give him a chance. Just meet for a drink and see how things went. I didn't say yes. I didn't say no. I wanted to, but I still had to play the game of 'always leave them wanting more' and all that crap.

I finally finished the call, sat down and gave it some thought. He definitely made me feel good. That in itself felt like half the battle. I felt comfortable and warm at the thought of him and I had not felt like that in a very long time. I got into bed with thoughts of potential running around in my head. I wondered if he was thinking of me too. Suddenly my phone pinged. It was him. I smiled to myself. Pretty smooth. Texting me fifteen minutes after we had just spent two hours on the phone. It was a video clip. I clicked into it. For a second or two, I couldn't quite work out what it was. Then I realised. With his phone in one hand and his knob in his other, he had filmed himself wanking and had sent it to me. Not just a general wank. No. He had filmed the last vital seconds of a wank and sent it to me.

I was floored.

I would love to tell you that I deleted the clip and never contacted him again, but sadly that was not the case. I can only blame my lowered expectations, but for some reason I just accepted it. After the various other penis shots I had received over time from potential dates, I started to see it as normal. Yes. Normal acceptable behaviour to send ejaculation videos to strangers who had given no indication that they wanted to receive them. Somehow, in my lowered sense of self, I now believed that raping my phone was fine.

So how did I respond? Well, I seem to remember responding as follows:

`Crikey.'

Well, what would you have said?

After that, I still continued to chat to him, but admittedly the innocence of our communications had been lost. I went along with it. I did start to refer to him as Bobby the Masturbator to my friends, but he was still a nice chap. He just now talked more about bending me over various pieces of furniture.

I can't lie, though. I liked a couple of the pictures he sent me. They came through while I was sitting at work. Honestly, you would be surprised how many of the rudey pictures I received whilst I was sitting at work. Anyway, it was two pictures he sent in quick succession. One was a selfie in his bathroom mirror, topless in combat trousers. The second was him in exactly the same pose only with his flies undone, holding his flaccid penis with his other hand. If I flicked quickly enough back and forth between the two pictures, it looked like a slightly disappointing erotic flick book.

I was still due to meet up with him the following Thursday. I know. I do not come across well out of all this.

But honestly, at this point, I was so lost in terms of what standard expectations should be when it came to dating that I just thought all the mobile phone soft porn was pretty normal. It's not that I am a prude, but I do think that you should probably have met the person at least once before you start telling them you are wanking over them and sending the proof.

Despite all the uninvited fluids, I was happy in my little world. Home life was good, work was fine, and I was quite happy to be meeting up with Bobby the Masturbator the following Thursday. It was the weekend of the football World Cup, and I was rooting for the Dutch. The weather was peachy and I had Helen staying for the weekend.

I woke up on Saturday morning to a few texts. There were a couple from Bobby. Something or other referring to my vagina. There was one other from a number that my phone didn't recognise. It had been sent at around 2am. It read:

```
'I know you might have consigned me to
the wanker bin, but if you still fancy
that drink I'd like to meet you.'
```

I had no idea who on Earth had sent it. I thought it might have been a comical mistaken text. You know, someone handing out a fake number which turns out to be a real number that just so happens to be mine. I just responded that I had no idea who it was and suggested that they might have been given the wrong number.

My phone pinged again. It read:

`'It's Michael. We were chatting a few months back and I bailed on meeting up.'`

Mr Marlboro Lights. Oh shit. Michael. I was completely flattered and completely pissed off in equal measures. It had been five months. How dare he assume that I was still single and ready to mingle? Didn't he know I was starting out on a beautiful relationship with Bobby the Masturbator? Hmm. When I thought of it like that, I had to admit to myself that I sort of was a bit single still. Bollocks did I want him to know that, though.

I let him try and explain why he'd bailed on me and why he'd never contacted me again. He was insistent that it was him, not me. He tried to tell me that he'd just bottled it. I got the chance to tell him how it had made me feel. And you know what? I felt better for it. As I said before, bailing on someone with no explanation is an exceedingly mean thing to do. A very mean, selfish thing to do to someone. With that in mind, I had no intention of giving him another chance.

Saying all that, it did make me feel a lot better. It was nice to know that he had always regretted his behaviour. By having the balls to send me that text after all that time, he had restored a little of the faith I had lost in dating those months before. Maybe he really was telling the truth and it was him (not me) after all.

I continued my day in the sunshine with Helen and Jessica. Happy in my little world. All of a sudden, the world of love and possibilities seemed a little bigger and a little more hopeful. Maybe not with Michael per se, but with someone out there. I had thoughts that I might not be so hideous and reminded myself that there are plenty of people out there with their own insecurities, too. Anyway, life was good. I had my family, my friends, my happy little life. Just knowing that someone felt so genuinely regretful about missing an opportunity to spend time with me made me feel so much better.

We had a quiet but fun night in on Saturday. I told Helen about Bobby. She wasn't hugely convinced, but she was happy if I was happy. Hey, who couldn't like his floppy penis flick photos? She did, however, ask about Michael, and I admit that at that point I did start thinking about him a bit more. Perhaps more out of curiosity than anything else. Still, I didn't think I could trust him. I felt that if I even entertained the idea of meeting him, I would be waiting for 'that' text again. I put my thoughts about him in a little box in my mind and moved on.

Sunday morning came and so did my voicemail alert:

'You have one new voicemail message from [number]. Seven minutes and thirty-six seconds.'

Now, I didn't know you could even leave voicemail messages that pissing long. It was Michael. He was on his way home from The Waterfront and had given me a call. He was pissed and had decided to leave me a message for as long as it took him to get from the club to the taxi rank. Highlights included his description of how you make cement: 'I think you need to mix water with ... umm ... cement'. He also stopped passers-by to get them to wish me: 'Happy four days after the 4th of July'. I know he was pissed – but hell, it was funny.

I played it to Helen. She literally laughed out loud listening to it. Not long after I had got up, I got an apologetic text from him. He was mortified. I found it hugely endearing and didn't mind one bit. Plus, at no point during his texts or pissed-up voicemail did he mention his cock / penis / balls / wanking / sex / spanking / bending over. It was a reminder that, unconventional as he was, there was still someone who was a bit of a gentleman out there.

We started sending a few texts that day and that evening. When Helen had left and Jessica was in bed, we texted each other all the way through the World Cup Final. I was rooting for Holland; Michael for Spain. He asked about meeting up again and I was hesitant. I mean, what would you have done?

So, after his third brave suggestion of meeting and heading off to the races, I relented. This time, I thought: bollocks to it. Although I suggested keeping it simple; part of the reason he had bailed the first time was that he had built it all up too much in his head. I suggested we just ripped off the plaster and met the next night for a cuppa. I admit that I was very silly and I would never ever recommend inviting some random dude you've sort of met over the internet round to your flat. But I did. I was lucky. Don't any of you be as silly as me. Of course, Jessica was away and my upstairs neighbour knew to call the police if she heard the sound of a chainsaw whirring, so I thought I had things reasonably well covered.

He was due round at mine at 8pm. At 7.40pm, my phone pinged. Oh, bloody hell. Not again. It was a text from him:

'Do you want me to bring you sausage and chips?'

Ah, the Casanova.

At 8pm on the dot, there was a knock at the front door. *Here we go*, I thought. It was an odd moment. My heart was beating faster than an acceptable resting rate, but other than that I felt ok about it. I paused for just a moment, turned the key and opened the front door. There stood a chap in jeans and a t-shirt, clutching a packet of Fox's Crunch Creams.

I invited him in. He perched on the end of the sofa nervously. I offered him a drink. He asked for tea. There we were. He was at one end with his mug of builder's finest, I was at the other end with my glass of Australian red. It felt a bit weird for a few moments, but luckily I am a talker. A nervous talker, maybe, but a talker all the same. Before long, he was sitting back and I was turned towards him, gibbering away with my feet tucked under me. I can't tell you what we talked about for those four hours on that sofa, but I can tell you how I felt. It was like talking to a friend. A tall, dark, attractive friend. He was self-deprecating and funny. Sweet and complimentary. In those four hours, there was no weird sexual undertone. No requests to photograph my lady garden. No asking to smell my neck. He didn't set my gaydar off. He didn't bring a knuckleduster. He didn't show me his Toblerone.

That night I lay in bed wondering what had just happened. As comfortable as I was, I had absolutely no idea if he fancied me at all. He gave me absolutely no indication whatsoever that he was interested in me in a romantic sense. I wanted to see him again. It was now the start of another waiting game.

Luckily, the wait was only until the next morning, when he asked me out again. Jess was away all week, so I accepted. Although I wasn't quite sure what capacity he was asking me out in, I liked him, and I was happy to spend another evening with Jambo81.

We decided on bowling. He picked me up at 7pm and we headed straight there. We had to wait for a lane, so we grabbed a drink. Well, I grabbed a drink. He went straight for the Deal or No Deal game. He was quite intense about it. I wouldn't say he ignored me, but I wouldn't say he said very much either. Super. I was out with a slot machine addict. It didn't get much better. Each time I went to bowl, I would turn back to find him with his back turned, getting a bowling ball. Great. A slot machine addict who took bowling seriously and didn't fancy me. Why was I even there?

After the game finished, we sat outside for a chat. He hardly looked me in the eye, let alone diving in for a snog. He asked me if I wanted to grab some food. It was getting late, so I invited him back for a Chinese. We ordered Chinese food. We ate Chinese food. It was nice, but that was about it. In all fairness, after the dates that I had put up with in the past, it was nice to sit with a chap and know he wasn't going to try and shove his hand in my pants without invitation.

Just before he left, I felt like I had to say something. No, not about whether he fancied me or not, but about whether he knew I had a child. Not that it should matter, but by the way he spoke, I got the distinct impression that he had no idea. You have to bear in mind that I had pictures of Jess in my flat, that there were toys in the corner of the living room, and that he had seen my Facebook pages with pics of Jess and me together. His response? 'Oh. Ok. I thought she was your niece.'

To make things that bit more awkward, as he was leaving I stopped him and leant in for a kiss. I had to know if he was interested, and this was going to seal it. I wished I hadn't. We awkwardly clashed teeth like two fourteen-year-olds. I was mortified. What the hell was wrong with me? It was similar to that awful teeth clash with Frank. Dear oh dear. He left and I knew I was never going to hear from him ever again. Hey ho.

But funnily enough, I did.

And it was fantastic.

He hadn't known I had a daughter, but he wasn't fazed. What looked to me like confusion was really indifference. He did fancy me. His 'legendary awkwardness', as he calls it, was what was stopping him from trying anything. The slot machine was just his way of making conversation. Each time he seemed to turn away after I bowled, he was actually turning away after watching my bottom as I bent over to bowl. After the tooth clash, he drove home hitting himself on the forehead, frustrated with his ineptness. He was an inept Love Soldier himself.

It's funny how when you see things from the other side, it all makes very different sense. That weekend, he came over for drinks and food. It wasn't long before he was at my end of the sofa and I was snug in the nook of his armpit. Safe in the nook of his armpit. Safe.

It wasn't all plain sailing for us in those early days. It probably would have been, but I was still understandably wary. I did act like a bell-end, but I had to be sure. When we were first together, I told him I was still dating someone else. Bobby the Masturbator, no less. Ha. Of course I wasn't, but I needed to know that he was willing to hang about. Not only that, but we didn't have sex for ages. In fact, it was the longest I had waited to have sex with anyone. Six weeks. Wow. I know. With my track record too. Six whole weeks. I didn't plan it like that, but it was another level of reassurance. He wasn't just there to part my legs. Don't get me wrong – it was worth it. I might have wanted to feel safe and loved, but come on – I wanted someone decent in the sack who had a nice willy, too.

I wanted to know everything about him. I wanted my friends to like him. I told Lisa all about him. She was away at the time. She suggested a list of questions for me to pose to him on her behalf. Lisa was only joking, but I forwarded them to him anyway. I thought it was worth sharing with you, particularly noting the references to my unsuccessful dating past.

From: MICHAEL
Sent: 26 July
To: Olwen
Subject: RE:

Hello there, Miss! On to the questions...

1) Is he employed? Does he have a salary?
Self-employed driving instructor, so as you told me I sit down all day taking money from kids. When I set up my own driving school, that will definitely be on my business cards!

2) Does he have 34000574836254758 other children by 38562563454 different women?
No, although me and my housemate once looked after a hamster for a very stressful couple of weeks. Until that moment I didn't realise how noisy hamsters could be in the middle of the night. I also learnt that when you tell off a hamster it doesn't listen!

3) Has he ever worn a life jacket?

Hmmm, had to think about this one. I went canoeing a couple of times so guess I must have.

4) Has he ever sent a video of himself masturbating to someone he's seeing?
No, I can never hold the camera still enough. Takes a special talent.

5) Does he take time off work 'sick' in order to get stoned with fat friends?
No. The last time I got stoned I thought I was getting stalked by pixies, so I decided to steer clear.

6) If 'yes' to no 2: Do any of his children eat like pigs?

7) Does he like Miniature Heroes himself?
Any chocolate is good! Except Turkish Delight and liqueurs.

8) Does he have any tattoos? If yes, are any of them the names of parents, pets or children?
No tattoos. Had a nipple pierced while drunk, but removed it at the earliest opportunity!

9) Has he ever worn beige trousers or a medallion?

No medallion, but I did once own a pair of beige flared cords. No matter what people told me at the time or any opinions since, I was cool! They were very tight, though, and quite uncomfortable. But these are the sacrifices us cool types have to make.

10) What are his views on slip-on shoes?
Good with a suit, but I prefer a nice Chelsea boot!

11) Are scarves for winter, or for fashion?
Winter. Anyone who wears one during the summer should be forced to spend winter in shorts and flip-flops. Same goes for beanies!

12) Has he ever bred dogs?
No. Have you been out with someone who breeds dogs? Was he a gypsy?

13) Would he grope you obnoxiously in front of your friends and family?
No. My legendary awkwardness would prevent me even if I wanted to!

14) Has he seen *Moulin Rouge*? Which character would he like to play in *The Sound of Music*?

Yes, once, round yours. If I'm being honest, not my favourite film, but also not as bad as I expected. As for the *Sound of Music* character, after some thought and consideration, I would like to be the uncle. Was it Uncle Max? If I remember, he had an awesome tache!

15) What are his views on Madonna?
No interest in Madonna. Good at what she does but not my cup of tea.

16) If he was to (accidentally) vomit on your parents' carpet, which of the following would he do in order to rectify the situation? a) apologise immediately to your mother and ask for a bucket and cloth to clean it up himself   b) creep back to your room and whisper to you that he'd had an accident   c) break the hoover.
Haha, I love the hoovering up the vomit story. As for me, I would probably go and hide in a cupboard and have a little man-cry for a few minutes and then pluck up the courage to own up to your mum.

17) What football team does he support?
Oh dear ... I'm afraid to say I'm a Manchester United fan. I do have genuine reasons for supporting them, but you are fully justified in mocking me for being a southern glory-hunting ba*@$rd.

go. I understood that the reality of love was far more beautiful and comforting that anything I could have imagined.

A few months into our relationship, Michael was due to go on holiday with his friends to Spain. It had been booked before we'd met. I dug deep and bound and gagged my inner insecure me. I pushed her deep down inside. I wanted him to go. I wanted him to have a good time. Most importantly, I wanted to trust him and to be honest, I did.

A few days before he was due to go, we had a tiff. I have absolutely no idea what about, but I suspect it was my inner insecure bitch squeezing to get out – mixed with a helping of good, old-fashioned PMT. That night, I felt thoroughly off. I thought I had indigestion, but I couldn't quite place it. I had a Babybel and some milk and tried to get to sleep. I was in a fair bit of pain, but the pain eased when I sat on the loo, so I just put it down to indigestion.

Thinking it was probably my ulcers playing up, I popped to the walk-in centre the next day. Well, it was no wonder the Babybel hadn't helped. I had appendicitis. Michael came straight down to meet me. No hesitation. He took me straight to the hospital as instructed. We sat together waiting for my hospital bed. Michael kept me distracted, and together we tried not to notice the poor chap having a loud explosive poo in the loo next to the waiting room. Ah, farting. Always funny. Eventually, I was taken to a bed. After an examination, I was told I was down to be operated on the next morning.

Without hesitation, Michael told me he wasn't going to leave me. I urged him to go to Spain, as I knew I would be ok. I was genuinely worried that his friends might think I had gone and got appendicitis on purpose to ruin his holiday. Look, I never said I was logical. I hated the idea that I was messing up his fun times. I would be ok. I knew I had my best friends if I needed them and that Jessica's dad would look after her. I would be fine. He still refused. This chap wasn't going anywhere.

When I was wheeled around the corner after recovery, I saw a white-faced Michael waiting for me. Unbeknown to me, the operation had taken three times as long as planned, as there had been a complication. I was fine, but the poor chap hadn't been told anything as he wasn't my next of kin.

I was discharged from the ward the next day with instructions regarding medications and how to deal with the wounds. Michael took me home. Later that evening, I wanted a proper wash, but I couldn't get my bandages wet. Michael ran a two-inch bath for me. Trust me: there is no sexy 'holding in' of your stomach when you've just had abdominal surgery. Michael didn't care. He sat next to me in the bath and washed my hair, careful not to hurt me and careful not to ruin the bandages, just as the doctor had instructed. He should have been sitting in a bar in Spain in the midst of a week-long piss-up with his mates. Instead, he chose to be there to look after me. Me and my saggy belly.

And that was when it hit me. Before that moment, I thought I loved him. In fact, at my thirtieth birthday party a few weeks earlier I had got massively pissed, proclaimed my undying love for him and then denied it all the next day. That moment was something different. I felt something else. A flash of deep, burning Elvis Love. And the feeling of pure security. I didn't ever want to let him go. I knew I would love him and be loved by him forever. It wasn't fireworks, rose petals, thunderbolts or champagne. It was two inches of lukewarm bathwater that finally clinched it. I had found my Love.

I realise now that love is not the same for everyone. We each have to go down our own paths. Some people find their someone at the end of their street, hardly needing to search at all. Some of us have to go around the world and suffer our own heartbreaks. Love is a game of chance. If you take one thing from reading my little book, please let it be that you might be a tiny bit more willing to take a chance. You cannot change the past, and if you could, you bloody shouldn't. Your past makes you a wonderful fuck-up. I learnt that True Love was most definitely a phrase suited best to musicals and cartoons.

Contented Love is a shitload better.

Conqueror

'Aaaand ... smize!'

Another weekend, another brunch, another comedy selfie session. The four of us do like doing a Tyra Banks while we are waiting for our food to arrive.

It is six years, almost to the day, that Michael stood nervously at my front door. Do I still feel the same way about him as I did when I was sitting in that bath? No. I can't say that I do.

Then I loved Michael, the man who looked after me. Now I love Michael, the man who loves me back just as much as I love him. Michael, the doting stepdad to my phenomenal daughter. Michael, the committed dad to our incredible son. Michael, the provider. The carer. The lover. My husband.

Do I wish I had met him earlier? Not really. Just to roll out another cliché, without my Love Soldiering I wouldn't be who I am today. I learnt so much. I learnt about myself and about others. It's a crazy world out there, but you have to believe. You have to keep the faith. So often things that seem like a disaster are really little blessings in disguise, taking us towards safety or true happiness. Have you ever listened to Radio 2 in the morning? They have a section called 'Pause for Thought'. A religious figure tells a little tale or moral for you to ponder on over the day ahead. One morning, on my way to work, I was listening to the radio on my headphones. Pause for Thought came on. I have listened to so many over the years, but this one truly stayed with me. The chap was referring to the Twin Towers disaster. 9/11. He repeated stories of the near misses. One person was wearing new shoes that had given her blisters and had to stop at a pharmacy, thus making her late. Another was having an awful morning culminating in her son throwing up his breakfast on her. She had to get changed, which made her late for work. All of the anecdotes he repeated were of people who had thought they were having a rubbish day. Those issues and incidents that hindered them ultimately saved their lives, as they weren't in the towers at the time the planes hit. The thought was that you should try and embrace times that you think are disastrous, as you never know where they are leading you. It might just be the path that saves your life.

    In the context of Love Soldiering, the bad experiences are there for a reason. There are times that you might consider just settling for the not-so-great. You might just completely despair. Remember that without those experiences, you won't find your Love Conquering destiny. Without the not-so-great decisions and dates, I wouldn't have my daughter – and I definitely wouldn't have walked down this path. My path led me to my True Love and happiness.

Keep the faith, Love Soldiers. Embrace the good and the not-so-good. Try not to regret the not-so-great choices; they make you the Love Soldier that you are.

You know what? I definitely don't regret a thing.

Acknowledgments

Thank you to everyone who took a risk and went on a date with me. Without you, I would know far less about myself and would have a much more limited supply of comedy anecdotes.

Karen, you're superb. Only I would have an editor who would send a picture of a potato to motivate me.

Without the encouragement and support from my amazing friends and family, I wouldn't have had the balls to write. Particularly Lucy, Paula, Kathryn, Rachel, Sy, B, Michael, Je, Mandy, Sarah, Eloise, Marie and Catherine – thank you all.

A big thanks to my bro and sister. Over the years you've both helped your inept little sister out so much. Mum and Dad, I know you continue to worry what the hell I am going to come up with next. Thank you for being the fab parents that you are, for trusting me and for knowing that I will always be fine.

My babies. Without you, I would be nothing. My Jambo81. Thank you from the base of my bones for supporting me with this little tale. A lot of husbands would have gone bananas. You showed me that I was right to believe.

www.ingramcontent.com/pod-product-compliance
Lightning Source LLC
Chambersburg PA
CBHW031543040426
42452CB00006B/169